How To Change
Your Life
By
Sitting
On
Your Butt

We wish you all the best of life!

XOXOXO

Beverlee

by Steve Ring
Illustrated & Designed by Julie Ann Stricklin

www.**SittingOnYourButt**.com

TEXT Copyright © 2008 STEVE RING
PROJECT EDITOR: Connie Rawlins
CONTENT EDITOR: Vera Caccioppoli & Hi-Way Haven: A Creative Hub for Writers
ILLUSTRATIONS & GRAPHIC DESIGN: Julie Ann Stricklin

NOTICE OF DISCLAIMER: The information contained in this book is based on Steve Ring's experiences and opinions. Steve Ring and the publisher will not be held liable for the use or misuse of the information in this book.

LLCN: 2008909965
ISBN: 1-4196-8904-5
BookSurge Publishing

To order additional copies, please contact BookSurge Publishing
www.booksurge.com

1-866-308-6235

Right now is an important moment.

Preface

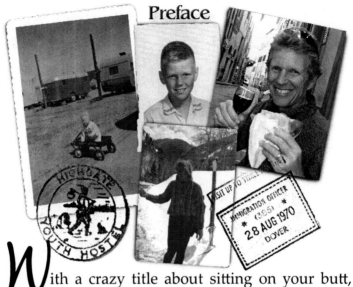

With a crazy title about sitting on your butt, you've got to be wondering—who is this guy? Well I have no credentials except what I've done in my life. I put together the lessons I've learned and the concepts are simple and effective. I've shared them with some of the real estate professionals who work for me. They know me and appreciate the success I've had and the life I lead. They thought I ought to write a book.

I've written this to be a handbook. One for you to carry around, make notes, underline and refer to every day. Hopefully when you need inspiration, you'll open it up, rather than reading the magazines at the checkout stands that tell you who just got pregnant. Use this book to remind yourself of what's really important.

I like this idea of sitting on your butt. There are many times each day when there is nothing better. It just feels good. **It will change your life.** And I mean making big or little changes. You get to decide. I'm going to show you how. It's a simple process and it takes a small effort. You can do it! Anybody can! Don't let life take over and run you over. Take control of your life like I did. You be the director of your life. Create the life you want by sitting on your butt.

In order for you to appreciate the things I will share with you, it may help to know more about me and how this process shaped my life before I even understood it. I might also tell you some stories just because I feel like it. I want this book to be fun and rewarding for both of us. I'll share what lessons I've learned as I stumbled along. Then I'll have some advice and concrete suggestions on how to have a better life. In later chapters, I'll show you how to get motivated and stay that way. Then I'll explain the simple process of changing your life by sitting on your butt. Then it's up to you. So get comfortable and dive in!

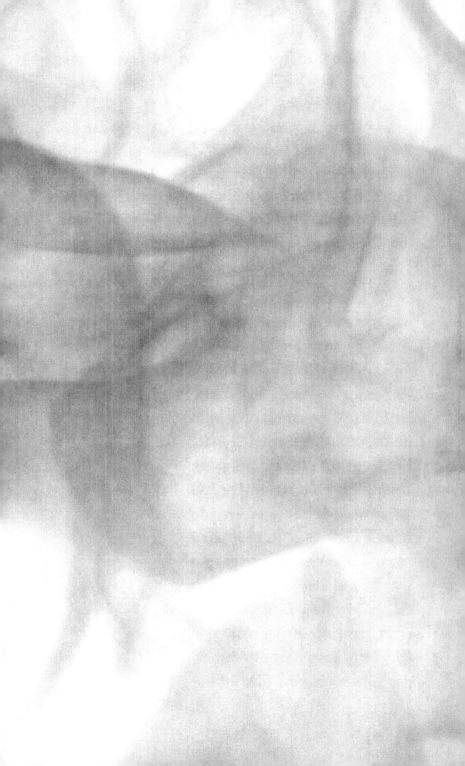

Chapter 1   **Learning To Pay Attention**

*B*efore I get started rambling, I have to make something clear and get it out of the way. If I don't, I'll get to the end of the book and my wife will be mad at me. I can't have that, it wouldn't be prudent. She has had a great deal to do with whatever positive changes I've made over the years. You need good feedback and a sounding board. She has done that and always supported me. So, *"thank you Beverlee!"*

Now when I say this part is all about me maybe you'll forgive me. I hope you'll find the lessons I learned helpful and worthwhile. I'll try to keep this part shorter than a novel.

Once upon a time (1950's), in a land far away, (Michigan) I grew up. It was a great place to grow up. Well I don't know if I grew up, but I did get older. I learned some good things and some things that held

me back. Some things I will remember out of order in my life. I'll try not to make anything up. It's my memory and I'm sticking to it. (My memory is a little better now, remind me to tell you why later). I was told

I was born in Mishawaka Indiana in 1950. I think my parents were gypsies.

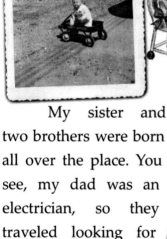

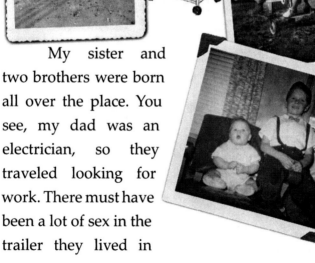

My sister and two brothers were born all over the place. You see, my dad was an electrician, so they traveled looking for work. There must have been a lot of sex in the trailer they lived in

9

because there were 4 of us. Naturally, they settled in a trailer park where there was plenty of work nearby. It seemed like an upgrade from a gypsy to a trailer park.

As a little kid, I remember having lots of fun. I was the human equivalent of a butterball turkey. I started out on my back yearning for the day when I had enough stomach muscles to sit up on my butt. It

took me a long time to sit up. When I got up I was in no hurry to walk. I was too chubby anyway. I think I became an expert (at an early age) at taking advantage of Butt time. I started to learn my first lesson. *Be happy and enjoy yourself no matter what you are doing, even if you're a butterball. What's important is what you decide happiness is. Don't let someone else decide it for you.*

My mom used a common birth control method at the time. She thought if you're nursing a baby you won't get pregnant. My sister was born one year after me and I didn't get to suckle as long as I wanted. (A guy can

never have too much suckling.) I think the butterball aloneness factor started to creep in and off I would crawl to be by myself. It must have been quite a sight but I did finally learn to walk.

My parents decided it was time to be non-gypsies, to settle down and build a life. They bought a couple of acres and started slowly to build a house. My dad worked on it after work and on weekends. He traded his electrical labor for others specialties when he couldn't do it himself. The relatives came and helped. It was cool. He even let my older brother climb on the roof and attempt to pound in nails. That was quite a sight for me because I could only go halfway up the ladder (it was the law). I didn't like heights anyway so that suited me just fine.

The house got finished and I continued to practice being a loner. I remember having a sandbox on our back patio and retreating there for hours to play. To earn extra money, my mom did day care. I didn't like it. I didn't want to share my mother or my sandbox.

My best friend was myself. I liked him, he always did what I wanted and we always had fun. I liked playing with myself (in those days, you could go blind from that). I liked being alone because it was easy. I wasn't very outgoing so it was easy to sit alone on the bus, in the cafeteria or not to be too friendly in school. When you don't say much, kids think you're stuck up.

All I knew was I didn't like some things about me and I didn't know how to change. If only I knew then what I know now. ***When you want change, think and do the opposite of what first comes to mind. My thoughts of always wanting to be alone, needed to be replaced on the spot by forcing myself to be around people. I know now that the short-term discomfort would have been replaced by the rewarding experiences.***

Let's lighten up here. The longer you live, the more you appreciate simple pleasures. Talk about simple. One of the things I remember fondly and with undiminished wonder, was how green and thick the grass always was over the septic tank. I didn't understand it nor did I really try to. It was just impressive. Or the time we took a pussy willow (I love that name) stick (and I mean small one) and shoved it in the ground in our front yard. No planting mix, no hole, nothing. That sucker grew up to be one big handsome tree. And if you know pussy willows like I know pussy willows, that's a pretty tree when it buds and blooms.

There is one thing that "took the cake" or "won hands down" (or up or sideways). I still remember how much I loved certain weather conditions. Sometimes in the winter it would rain, just at freezing temperature. Then the rain would freeze on the trees and on the snow. I loved seeing the clear ice frozen on all the

tree branches. Best of all was walking to school when every step crunched under my feet. It's heaven, until it melts. *Why do we get too busy to enjoy these moments as we get older? We need to work on that one, right now!*

When we're growing up, dads teach us lots of things. Things we can use and things it takes a while to get rid of. My dad taught me the value of hard work and taking responsibility. I got that from osmosis because he hardly ever said a word unless forced. In fact, my mom forced him to be the enforcer. You know, the one with the leather belt across the butt. (The very one I liked sitting on.)

My mom used to always tell me how he felt. *13* Things like "you know he loves you" and "you know he doesn't like using the belt" and "it even made him cry". Then there was "wait till your dad gets home". I thought I'd just sit on my butt and enjoy it while I could. I usually didn't have to wait long because my dad left for work very early (early to me anyway) and came home early. He'd take care of business if that was on the agenda or do his normal routine. Clean the kitchen counters and sink, have a snack, sit in the easy chair and read the paper, doze off, take a shower, then eat dinner.

I would sometimes try to force him to help me with homework, which he reluctantly did. Never

did he say much and mostly when pressed into action. My mom filled the talking gap. She also made the big excuse "he's doing the best he can". Yes that was true. *It was also true that change takes effort, and making a consistent effort to change is the only way to change. To do anything less is the easy way out.*

We lived on the outskirts of town. The elementary school, which we could see from our dining room, was an easy walk. Nobody had fences so naturally we would take a straight line to school right through all our neighbors yards. When we got older, we took the bus to junior high. Each morning we would watch (from the same window) for the bus, then the shout went out, "The bus is coming!", and we raced out the door down the long driveway to the unpaved street. Nobody seemed to ever want that road paved. I'm glad it wasn't for several reasons. It felt more like we were out in the country, off the beaten path.

One day my friend and I are riding down a hill on the same bike with him sitting on the center bar. I asked him to use the brake to slow us down because I couldn't reach it. He squeezes the front brake. It wasn't pretty and it took a few minutes to clean the gravel out. Still it was better than hitting asphalt. (Besides, they didn't even make helmets then, nor were seat belts used).

Riding the school bus was always interesting too.

You had time to watch the world go by. It was nice because the ride wasn't long and the bus was always half empty. Unheard of today!

From that same window we could also spot the mailman coming from a distance. I ran out one day and walked around the front of the mail truck, grabbed the mail out of the box and stepped back in front of the truck. The mailman stepped on the gas and knocked me on my ass. Both of us were stunned and embarrassed. I got right up, said I'm okay and walked back to my house. *I decided I was going to pay more attention to what I was doing. You get much better results at anything when you*

pay attention. It's harder to get better when the things we do are unconscious.

We were a traditional household. After school my sister did the dishes, and started supper because my mom got a full time job. (The three boys didn't do chores until the weekend). I had a favorite snack after school. Put butter on 2 slices of bread, brown sugar on both, throw in a banana and it's a sandwich. Yum. I hated the dentist. I was there way too often. At least he did a good job because I still have all those fillings.

Did everyone else's parents do this too? My mom would drop us kids off at church, go home, come back and pick us up later. I figured out how to get my brother and sister inside then I sat outside enjoying the great outdoors. (Good butt time.)

I always enjoyed my quiet time, time alone, time to think. I don't know where this came from but I started to think about how I would be a millionaire some day. I also saw myself being a manager or running things. I had no idea how I would do that and of course I had no idea about inflation. You know, a million ain't what it used to be.

I had no idea that holding thoughts in your head over time makes them come true. Maybe some regular quiet time by yourself is a good thing. You end up getting what you want.

I had a pet rabbit named Princess. I kept her in a cage in the back yard. Rabbits are dumb. I liked her a lot anyway. All she did was hop around, eat, pee &

poop little pellets. Too many of them. Cleaning the cage even outdoors wasn't any fun.

Oh I forgot one thing. She was real good at once in a while making a male rabbit real happy. Somehow my mom knew when it was time to take her down the street to our neighbors garage where she was left overnight with the local stud. At my age, I was a little in the dark myself. Sure enough, without fail, my little girl would soon have a bunch of babies. Then I got to sell them like most kids sell lemonade. That was fun.

When it came time to talk to me about the birds and bees (aka: sex) my mom was unanimously chosen by my dad. It wasn't easy for her to get started so I tried to make it easy to finish. I already heard all about it on the school bus. What a relief for her. I remember thinking at the time, why call it the birds and the bees. I can't imagine them having sex. Or maybe that was the idea. To keep it clean. I'm also thinking that I'm into rabbits, and rabbits love to have lots of sex, so why aren't innocent little rabbits used to explain the deed?

I used to love to stay with my grandparents for a couple of weeks each summer. Grandma made me go to church with her on Sundays. It wasn't my favorite thing but it sure was interesting to watch the people.

I always liked the food she made, probably because it was so different. She cooked it to death in a pressure cooker. I don't know anyone who uses those

things anymore. It always looked so dangerous to me, like it could blow at any time. It reminded me of those water rockets that we would pump up and they would shoot straight up in the sky. I was always fascinated by things flying in the air.

The best part was the time I spent working with my grandpa. He always had me fetch the tools he needed. After several trips back and forth, I finally brought the right one. Then we would do my favorite thing. Take a break and drink an ice-cold Nesbitt orange drink.(My wife doesn't understand why I occasionally like to buy an orange drink.)

The other thing I loved was when my grandpa would take me out with his truck, tractor and trailer and do landscaping jobs. I got to sit up on the fender of the Ford tractor as he did his work. He talked to me. He never got impatient with me and I loved how he seemed always to be in good spirits. *"Even-keeled" they would say. I decided I wanted to be like that.*

Somewhere along the line I forgot to mention that I didn't remain a butterball for long. I guess I decided to do something besides eat. From then on they said I was thin. They say it's easy for me because it's probably in the genes. Maybe it is to some degree. What I remember is feeling uncomfortable if I put on weight. When I did, I became suddenly conscious and aware of what I was eating. Then I cut back until I felt good again. It was a built-in governor. It's a lot easier than exercising

and it works better. *As a matter of fact, sitting on your butt works better than exercising, because it's all about what's in your head. Everything you accomplish always starts there. (I'll explain this later.)*

I was a cub scout then a boy scout. I liked both. There was always a sense of adventure and learning.

My mom was a den mother and when I was an adult, I was a den master. It was a great excuse to do more camping out. That was fun.

I even went to boy scout camp as a kid. All the boys wore neckerchiefs with slides as part of our uniform. We had a carving contest for those slides. I spent some time coming up with my idea, then hours carving and painting.

I thought my 3-inch wooden matchstick slide turned out really well, I was excited for the judging. I took my defeat (2nd place) kinda hard. I had lost to a scout who took a bar of soap, cut a hole in the middle and stuck it on his necktie. I was thinking, how about a good rainstorm right now and we'll see whose holds up. No such luck. I learned more from 2nd place.

Life's not always fair and the only thing I can control is my reaction to whatever happens. That remains, to this day, one of the biggest and most important lessons I try to teach to everyone who will listen.

Homework wasn't so bad most of the time. The part I struggled with the most was when we were asked to be creative and come up with an idea for a project. Doing it was no problem, thinking of it was hell. I always had to turn to my mom. We'd eventually come up with something.

When I had children, they turned to me for help. Over the years I had learned something that made it a lot easier for me. Now people would say I'm pretty creative and I can do it fairly quickly. *I learned that*

by sitting quietly, and closing my eyes, I could let my mind wander and it would start coming up with ideas. By sitting on my butt and not trying too hard, it actually worked better.

21

I graduated from selling bunnies to selling University of Michigan football tickets. Some call it scalping. It wasn't. We sold them for face value or less. We would start a half mile away from the stadium, buy extra tickets from fans, then move closer to the stadium and resell them. We'd make a $100 on a good day plus get to go and watch the game free. Then we'd get fired up and go play touch football after the game. It was the best of times.

The real skill was talking everyone into letting me play quarterback or receiver. Who the heck wanted to block, I wanted the glamour positions. I wasn't that good. The secret was to be a little bit better than the others. Mostly I just thought I was and that was just enough. *I was starting to learn that how you think about things, and what you believe you can do, has a huge effect on the outcome.*

Either I had the entrepreneurial spirit or I was too shy to look for a job. I gravitated towards doing things where I was in charge and could make some money.

I liked making money and didn't mind working hard for it. (I didn't say smart.) I started with a newspaper route. I would get home from school, fold newspapers so I could throw them, load them in a rack in the front of the bike and a rack on each side of the back wheel and then get a push to get launched. Staying upright was a "whole 'nother ball game". Actually, it was kinda fun in perfect weather. In bad weather, I had to walk. Just try walking with two gigantic bags full of newspapers hanging each way from your neck. (It might have been okay if I had been raised a Sherpa.)

The good and bad thing was the route included my neighborhood. Nice to be close to home. Not nice when each home had a 100-foot driveway and between each house was half a city block. That's a dumb choice

when you get paid by the paper. I did learn to take responsibility. I had no choice, they never stopped the presses. I think it was my mom's favorite job too. She loved it when the weather was really bad (Michigan- no way!) and she had to drive me through the route as I delivered to each door. Squeezing it between her job and dinner was the part she really loved. (not!)

Then there was Christmas when some people were nice and gave me a tip. Each Christmas I would wonder if all the others even thought for a second what I went through to get a newspaper to them and how little I must be paid for it. Maybe that's why two years was all a carrier could handle.

Now I wonder if it's bad if I don't tip my newspaper carrier who has to get up early each day, rain or shine and drive his car throwing the paper out the window? I'm conflicted. There's no hesitation when it comes to tipping restaurant help. My wife and I are generous to a fault. They work hard and they can't make a living without tips. Maybe we need to stop being so damn busy, and just for a minute think of how everyone else feels. Someone has to do all those jobs and they need to be treated with dignity and respect. *If you're glad they're doing the job and not you, then all the more reason to be kind and generous.*

Somewhere around 1966, my mom made a mistake that haunted her and my dad for years. She

owned one of the simplest cars ever built after WWII. A Volkswagen Beetle. Also known as a VW bug or just VW. Four speeds. Slow, slower, slower in a wind and very slow up a hill. Forty horsepower of pure muscle, with little or no ability to heat the car up in the winter, or defrost the windows. Nonetheless, off Mom went to work each day until the engine blew up.

Here was her mistake. She gave me the car. (Good excuse to stop freezing her ass and let me freeze mine instead.) If I could figure out how to fix it, I'd have myself a car. A buddy and I took the engine out and took it apart. What a mess but the problem was obvious. Now two things set the stage for the future.

A VW sitting in our 100′ driveway on blocks and a torn-apart engine in the basement. I could thrill both parents at once! The engine was so simple I could fix it even using scavenged parts from the junk yard. So I started almost three years of rebuilding the engines for customers charging $100 each. They always ran no matter what I did and I always had spare parts left over; (I could never figure out how that was possible). During that time I also bought and sold VW bugs and VW buses making sure I always had 2 – 3 vehicles lining our driveway, in various states of repair. Between all the hard work, my buddy (who I bribed to work all day for a Whopper lunch at Burger King) and I would turn demolished VW's into makeshift dune buggies. Our version was an engine on a frame with seats. We would have a grand old time racing around our two acres and the many open fields beyond our subdivision. It was especially exciting at night without headlights. Thirty to forty mph is fast when you can't see anything. How do you spell "seat belts"?

I don't want you to think I never worked for someone else because I did. I pumped gas at the local Sinclair station. Remember when someone washed your windows too? It was boring between pumping so I brought engine parts to work on. My boss wanted me to sit there and do nothing so he fired me.

I also worked at the A & P grocery store as a

bagger. Talk about boring. My manager promised to promote me to stocker (big money job). Months went by and we parted company. I felt bad because my mom helped me get that job.

Next I got a job at Xerox, the microfilm company. Fascinating technology. My job wasn't though: I sat in a darkroom unwrapping film all day.

Happily I was able to use my considerable mechanic skills (not!) to land a helper job at a garage. The owner was probably the biggest crook I ever knew. At least he was small time. I didn't like being a grease ball. Luckily I got to do other things that were exciting like driving big utility trucks across town. Half the time I couldn't even shift the damn thing.

One time I drove a gigantic truck so big that you could stand in front of it and the driver couldn't see you. I got the scare of my life (so far). That truck was so powerful I drove it with the air brakes on. It wasn't long before I had no brakes and couldn't stop and ran right through a stop sign. Talk about helpless. I wasn't worried about me. I was worried about running right over the top of any car I might hit. I missed the cross traffic and had my brakes back a ¼ mile later. This was not a dull job.

It was on this job that I finally got to see a grown man cry. My boss had just installed a beautiful 15' wood roll up garage door. It was his pride and joy. I was taking

a battery out of a truck parked right in front of it. I accidentally hit the starter with a wrench. The truck lurched forward, over and over and over and over again, battering that new door. I couldn't figure out how to stop it. My boss came running out and finally got it to stop. There was much cussing and tears in his eyes. I was fascinated by that truck. It had a mind of its own.

There's one last crappy job worth telling you about, and I mean crappy. The company made the crap holding tanks for RV's. I was a temp worker and the boss liked my work so he hired me as a regular. I was one of the few workers who could put these two pieces together so they wouldn't leak. In my mind it was a terrible design and I couldn't believe it would

hold up under the abuse. I water-tested them and if they didn't leak, off they went. This was another boss that didn't give a shit (pardon me) about customers. Sometimes I had to go out back and throw cardboard in the incinerator. That was actually a lot more fun. I got carried away. Too much cardboard! The ashes settled on the rejected holding tanks piled out back. They caught fire. By the time we put it out, most of them were damaged. I'll never forget my boss saying he was actually glad because he would report the tanks as ready to ship. Then they would get more money from the insurance company. I don't think I fully understood fraud. I did understand that I didn't want to be like the bosses I had. ***I hated the dishonesty. I vowed to be the opposite and always to be as fair as possible.*** I'm proud of that reputation I have as an adult. My parents certainly helped establish my core beliefs in that regard.

Oops. One more story about one more job. My dad got me a summer job as an electrician's helper. It was a union job and they paid me way too much for what I did. I was partnered up with a journeyman electrician. You know, one that knows what they are doing. Well mine didn't, on top of that he was a lazy son of a bitch. (I'm using construction guy talk here). We were assigned a job and as soon as we got away from the boss he tells me to get lost. Get lost for two

hours and don't get caught. He needed to go take a nap. That's what I call on-the-job training.

In high school, my ego started to get in the way. It's annoying. I don't think very much good usually comes from it. As I mentioned before, I always found ways to work and make money. I liked making it and I didn't mind working for it. So when I had enough money my ego insisted that I buy a beautiful, brand new, manly Triumph motorcycle.

I loved the sound it made. I had never ridden anything but a small motorcycle. A 650cc was a huge step up. "Are you sure you can handle this?" No problem, I told the salesman. "It's parked out front and it's all yours." Man was I cool now. It wasn't easy to start because you had to put all your weight down on one

leg to kick the starter. I got it started then realized how tough it was to hold up. It was heavy. I hit the throttle and the bike took off with me holding on for dear life. My hands barely held on and my legs went straight back. I looked like a scarf in a windstorm. Fortunately, the bike slowed down, I flopped on to the seat and regained control. I made it home without hurting the bike, myself or any humans. I did eat a few bugs until I figured out you have *to keep your mouth shut. (There's a lot of times when that would be good advice.)*

I used to love riding around town on my cool-sounding bike. I loved the freedom, (didn't fully appreciate the great gas mileage), the wind in my face and the open sky.

One little problem however, I was always so busy enjoying everything and looking around that I would forget I was on the road with cars. You know, cars that stop, start and turn. Sometimes they even signal directional turns. Most of the time in bad weather they don't know what they were doing. Anyway, cars had this annoying habit of stopping in the road in front of me. I had this annoying habit of not seeing them stop in front of me. I was an average rider at best and the first time this happened to me I lucked out. I quickly laid the bike down on its side and slid underneath the back of the car in front of me. For some unknown reason my back tire caught on the asphalt, the bike popped back up, and I rode around the outside of the car. Never touched it, I must have looked like a stunt rider when in fact I had no control at all of what happened. That'll get your heart pumpin'.

The next time I'm riding to school in the morning, minding my own business (not paying attention). Sure enough, a VW bug stopped in front of me. This time I thought I would try something different. I ran straight up the rear end of that bug, smashed it in and bent the hell out of my nice motorcycle. I was shocked to find out how much it cost to fix my bent forks. About this time I decided that things were not headed in the right direction. I'd better get rid of this motorcycle before I hurt someone else's car.

My ego was called upon again and my ego was happy to step up to the plate. I guess you could say "my head was screwed on backwards". I was raking in the big bucks and decided I needed a show car.

I found myself a jacked-up, gold Corvette, got

a small loan and she was mine. It was the American dream. A fancy car, monthly payments and "not a pot to pee in".

Once again, I thought I was pretty hot stuff. Surely the chicks would dig me now. Alas, no change. I did like driving it around and I learned how to wax it so it looked nice. (A VW wasn't worth waxing you know.) I left that Corvette at home when I went to college because they didn't allow first-year students to have a car.

By the second year, I had lost interest in my Corvette because I needed a VW so I could go skiing each weekend. So I sold the Corvette. I learned some lessons. *When your ego gets to decide what's important, it will cost you money and it will slow down your personal development. Our*

ego lusts after things to make it feel better which makes us think we feel better. It's only temporary and it's not real. I had enough of that. I wanted something better for myself.

I continued to be plagued by shyness throughout school. I talked when I was made to. Girls always liked me when I was a kid. I think it was the fine haircut my dad used to give me called the Princeton. He shaved off everything except a small clump of hair in the front that you didn't need to comb. My dad used to cut our hair in the basement in dead silence. I looked forward to those times of bonding.

Dating was challenging. I had to find a girlfriend that liked to talk. At least one that could keep up a conversation with just a few words from me now and then. Funny thing, but I married a gal just like that: only I had to double the number of words I spoke.

Anyway, I needed a little help getting a girlfriend. Exposure was the key. In ninth grade, I won a highly prestigious contest. There were a number of categories; however, I took the "best-looking" prize. I remember a friend saying, "I hope you don't get stuck-up now". I think she meant she hoped I would still talk to her because she wasn't considered in the "in crowd". She figured this prize would catapult me like a rocket into that group. Fat chance.

The door did open and I took one step in and looked around. There was a lot of ego flying around so

you had to duck a lot. Gossip was the language of choice. Staying "in" took effort and everyone had to do their part. The whole group was on a committee always silently voting on every person, every piece of clothing and every event. Talk about exhausting. I did my best but I didn't enjoy it. It was too fake. Everyone was insecure. It was easier on the "out" side.

While I was half in and half out, I caught the attention of a pretty little Jewish girl. She was my meal ticket. She was part of the "in crowd" already. Now the "in" crowd would have to put up with me and I didn't have to play the "in" games. I didn't have to pretend to be friends with any of them. That worked for me. She stayed my girlfriend for most of high school. That worked for me, except that it didn't make me learn to talk more and didn't teach me how to date.

In my senior year, I realized these things, and started to pull away. I knew that we were both going off to college somewhere different anyway. Her parents also went to bed every night praying that she wouldn't end up with me. They wanted a good Jewish boy and although they were pleasant to me, I could feel the underlying tension (aka: vibes). Don't let me get started on the problems of religion. Her parents should have been focused first on their daughter's happiness. If that turned out to be a Jewish boy, fine. If not, fine. *Why do we always try to control everything? Why is our way the only good way? What happened to flexibility?*

Chapter 2   Giving In To Adventure

*F*lying always fascinated me. Flying birds, planes, kites, whatever stayed up in the air. What made that work? I figured it out then did a science project in Jr. High. That project helped me get over any interest I might have had in cigarettes. It may sound strange, but many of my best lessons came from an unusual experience.

So here was my science project. I used a vacuum cleaner and about seven smoking cigarettes. I had a cross section of an airplane wing inside this box with a plexiglas cover. The smoke would come out of the jets and travel across the wing and demonstrate airflow. The problem was in the execution. The vacuum was one speed, full blast; the other was lighting seven cigarettes at once. I think I sort of got it to work twice at home. My teacher was impressed by the concept and wanted me to demonstrate it in class. No way. I didn't think it would work under pressure and I was sick of cigarettes already. Maybe we shouldn't fight it with kids. Just make them smoke seven cigarettes at once, that'll cure 'em.

I also have a method for preventing the start of a coffee-drinking career, (which by the way could

save someone enough to buy a house). My parents unwittingly sealed it for me. We were on a ski trip early in the morning, headed to the mountains. I was thirsty and the only thing to drink in the car for six people, was a thermos of black coffee. Okay I'll try it. I could not take more than a sip. I don't drink coffee to this day. Try it on your kids. Don't add the milk and sugar that makes it easy to drink and get in the habit. It's easier to not start than to quit.

Back to flying. We used to build model airplanes with paper stretched over balsa wood frames. Man they were fun to fly. Cheap thrills when we could get the little engines to run. If we could get two running at the same time, (rarely) we'd have dog fights in the sky. We'd tear up those crepe paper strands that we attached to the tails. It was always sad when we'd make a wrong move and the plane did a face plant. In for repairs, out the next day. I need to do that again. (Not the face plant part).

Of course the next logical step was I had to try real flying. In high school I took flying lessons. Every pilot will tell you what a thrill it is when your instructor tells you it's time to go solo. What, are you joking? I'm old enough to wreck a car, but a plane? To me, flying solo the first time was just like taking your first driver's test. Unpleasant, scary, nerve-wracking and then you're damn glad it's over with no damage done.

When you get your driver's license, you proceed to do dumb things every time you drive. Have you ever seen a kid drive defensively? No, its balls to the wall, get from here to there as fast as you can. You don't think about killing yourself or someone else. When you get in an airplane, you can't help but think of that. Funny thing is, it's actually safer. For me, Mr. Motorcycle, I'm not so sure.

One of the requirements after you soloed was to get more flight time with your instructor. That was then followed by a cross-country solo. A four-hour flight I had to chart and return from safely. It was exciting, especially the part where I got lost. They teach you to circle until you figure it out. I circled four times, looking up, then down over and over at the map. To my great relief, I did figure out where I was. Then I flew to

my destination airport, got my book signed off, and headed home. Your home field is always a welcome sight.

I didn't fly a lot because it was very expensive. I barely flew enough to keep my skills at an acceptable level. I thought they were good enough to fly three friends from college back to Ann Arbor, our home town. It was only about an hour away. Four guys with

their bags, under the weight limit but certainly two more people than I ever had in a plane at once. It was a smooth flight except for the landing. There was a cross wind (across the runway) and it was gusting. I approached as I usually would. We were about forty feet above the dirt runway when the red light flashed and the warning buzzer went off. It's called a stall. That means if nothing changes you're going down

fast because the wings have lost lift. My instincts had me push in the throttle and give the engine more gas. Fortunately, the engine responded quickly to full power and I flew out of danger, and back for another try. My friends of course were fine because they didn't know any better. I was scared to death. I learned under those conditions you need to land with more power. The second time was no problem.

Finally, I let too much time lapse between flying. Up I went to get reacquainted. Big mistake. This time I really thought I was going to die when the plane was slow (in my opinion at the time) in coming out of a stall from well up in the sky. I don't think I did what I had been taught. I couldn't get back to the airport fast enough. Hang up the license you slow learner. I don't fly anymore, but I did learn some other important stuff.

Sometimes the ability you feel you have in your head doesn't match up with reality. That could be a good thing unless you put yourself or others in danger. When you can picture being or having something before it becomes a reality, you're well on your way to it becoming true.

I've owned and driven a Porsche, Corvette, trucks and a bunch of other cars. My favorite one to drive was my VW bus. There was something magical about the steering and the ride. In  1968 I think I could say it was the favorite of hippies. Draft dodgin', sex lovin', drug lovin', music lovin', long hair lovin' and funny clothes lovin' hippies. I wasn't quite there yet but I did put a big peace sign on the front of my bus and let my hair grow a little. I liked the sex part. I found I preferred having it in the bus to having it in a VW bug. (Sex in the bug just felt a bit like a circus act!)

The VW bus was the vehicle of choice for cross

country trips. The one I liked had a camper built in with bed, benches and a sink. Sweet. The summer after high school, my buddy and I took a trip out west. He wanted to find a place to live so we went all over seeing the sights. We always picked up hippie hitchhikers. They were fun. Always characters. Rarely knowing or caring where they ended up. Real free spirits, male and female. They didn't mind eating our food. Sometimes we even camped out together overnight. With a full bus we were lucky to break 40 mph, but it was okay because no one was in a hurry. ***Aren't some of your best times when you're not in a hurry?***

My parents joined a small ski club. We used to take trips to the most popular ski resorts in Michigan. At the time the Boyne Mountain ski area was a favorite

with a whopping 600 feet of vertical drop. To get a feel for this size, that would be about two weeks trash piled up at your city dump. It was 60 seconds to ski down and 20 minutes in line. That's where my love of skiing started. (Not in line.) It was also fun hanging out in the lodge with the other kids.

It was in the day of rope tows and POMA lifts. The tow was tough on your hands, your arms and your legs. You couldn't let go till the top. It was funny to watch others on their learning curve. The spread eagle was always fun. People would have gloves, jackets, hats, poles, hair and false teeth pulled off. Then there

was the lucky one that had her jacket tangled up so she ended up hanging six feet in the air. The POMA lift was a big step up because you could relax, put the

pole through your legs and let it pull you up by your butt. Then came the chairlift, which was heaven, then the gondola which was even better. (Many years later.)

My enthusiasm for skiing continued, as I got older. My brother and I ended up getting pretty good by Michigan standards. You have to love skiing if you're going to hitchhike the 5-hour drive to the ski hills, in the middle of winter with your ski's. To save money, we'd ski without lift tickets and find some closet to sleep in free. One of our favorites was underneath a platform about three feet high. By taking off the 2X3 foot grill, we could crawl under and have a nice warm night. Then there was the excitement of sneaking around the ticket checkers. It usually worked pretty good. When there was too many of them, we would get tickets from people leaving for the day.

Once I was skiing with a buddy and we got caught. The ticket checker was walking us to the office. He didn't like how slow I was walking so he pushed me. I swung my ski poles at him and purely by accident (of course) hit him in the nuts. That's slang for where it hurts a lot. He bent over in some degree of pain and then decided to go get help. That was our chance to get lost and hide out. Once safe, we had our good, nervous laugh.

I continued skiing when I went to college. I went every weekend that I could. Finally I took a week long

trip to Aspen, Colorado with a ski club. First I made sure I didn't talk to anyone, then I made sure I didn't ski with anyone, then I made sure I sunburned the shit out of my face. I wanted a tan, so I closed my eyes and tilted my face towards the sun on each chairlift ride. I wanted to further speed up the process by not wearing sunscreen. Being fair skinned at 11,000 ft. high, that's not a good idea. The next day I was covered with blisters. Medical attention? Are you kidding, that cost money. I'll just ask at the drugstore. Maybe that white stuff people are wearing on their nose will work. (I wasn't about to not ski.) As painful as it was, and it was, I covered my face with white zinc oxide every day. Then every night wiped it off with toilet paper. That hurt worse. It was worth it just to be there skiing. I couldn't believe this place. Their bunny (beginner) hill was bigger than Michigan's biggest. I vowed to return. It was interesting to me then and it still is now. *We can put up with pain and discomfort if something else is more important. Whatever it takes we're willing to do, if we want something bad enough. If we could only channel this energy somehow.*

Of all the things I did during the hippie years of the 60's and 70's, it was the simplest and most innocent that landed me in jail. My brother and I were hanging around Salt Lake City one summer. We rode

our bikes and played tennis. We played on the campus of BYU. We also ate in the school cafeteria. We just walked in, took a tray, filled it up (over and over) and tried to blend in. That wasn't easy because our hair was longer and we weren't regulars. We got to eat several free lunches that way. One day after stuffing ourselves, we were greeted by the campus security police. Are you students? Ah, no. My brother, four years younger, got up and dashed out the exit. Oh, shit! I panicked, grabbed our tennis racquets (which he left behind) and ran the other way. After a half-hearted (full stomach) sprint across a grassy field, I was tackled by the officer, and handcuffed behind my back. I was then transferred to the SLC police department and stayed overnight

in jail. Nice lodging, and free. The VP of student affairs laid down the rules for dropping charges. Full restitution from both of us, a written apology and a personal appearance by my brother. All of that was finally arranged. $2.50 each and a chuckle from the VP.

Looking back, I realized some things. I didn't feel right about running away, so a man twice my age in hard black shoes ran me down in an open flat field. He wanted to catch me (highlight of his day) more than I wanted to get away.

Without realizing it, our emotions create motivation that far surpasses what we can generate by just trying consciously to do something. I think I had to sit on my butt for *a while to realize how really important that lesson was for me. (This will make more sense later.)*

There were two times when I should have gone to jail because I was caught but escaped. My brother and I were on one of our many trips cross the country in the VW bus. We were cruising along minding our own business, and smoking pot. (Aka: dope, marijuana, weed.) Mind you, we were only testing some stuff my

brother bought. And of course not inhaling (in case we want to run for political office). Anyway, the inside of the bus was full of smoke. All of a sudden traffic stopped up ahead. We found ourselves in a police checkpoint line, about six vehicles back. Now remember the peace sign on the front, two longhair hippie types, in a bus full of funny-smelling smoke, in Nebraska. Not a safe haven. Talk about panic. I'm driving so my brother laid down in the back like he's sleeping. (We don't need two more red eyes staring at the police.) We decided our only hope was to crack the window just enough to talk. I couldn't believe the officer paid no attention to me. I didn't fit the profile of the guy they were looking for. We escaped.

Despite what you've read so far, I'm a pretty responsible guy. It was a struggle for me when my brother or my good friend came up with an idea that caused a conflict in my head. I came up with a way that made it easier for me to decide what to do. *I asked myself if I would be likely to ever get the chance to do it again.* Even if I could, would it be as much fun without whoever I would be doing it with now. *I'm not talking about bad stuff. I'm talking about having adventures. The thing we seem less and less likely to have as we get older and settle in. The best times in my life seemed to be when I gave in to the adventure.*

Next lucky break, I was in college and I was in the middle of final exams. My buddies show up in a Pontiac convertible. They are going to Mardi Gras in New Orleans and they wanted me to go. That makes five of us crammed in this car for a nonstop 1000 mile drive through five states. I would miss two final exams and likely flunk. I asked myself the question, grabbed some clothes and off we went. I'll never forget what a great experience it was.

We still talk of the close call we had on the way back. Try to picture five hippie-like dudes driving straight through the conservative southern states. Guys were sleeping as best they could in the back seat. I never drove. One of the few times I sat up front (shotgun we called it) we were jarred from our traveling trance by a siren. We were being pulled over around dusk. We didn't know we had a taillight out. My friend yells to me to "hide the pot" and hands me a sandwich bag about one third full. Being the expert that I wasn't, I threw it under the bucket seat I was in. The police walked around the car, made us open the doors, and they hunched down and searched everywhere they could using flashlights.

To this day we still laugh about it. We still can't believe they didn't see the baggie. We would have been toast because they wanted to find something. (I'm your guy if you need something hidden.) My cool-headed

buddies tell me, after the fact, I should have hidden it in my pants. Sure. Hide their pot on me. (I survived to return and make up my final exams.)

I finished college and my brother finished high school. It was time to go to Aspen, Colorado.

I bought a rusted Ford pickup and we started to build a camper on the back. By late summer, my brother left on his bicycle, rode across Michigan then took the ferry over to Wisconsin. About 10 days later, I drove to Wisconsin and picked him up. We built the camper as we traveled. We barely got it enclosed by the time the snow flurries hit. (Did I tell you we had no

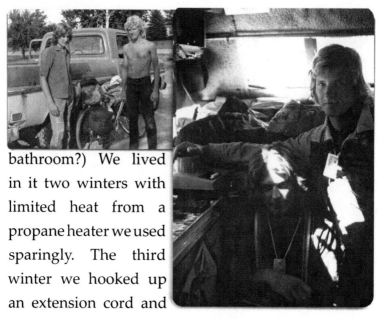

bathroom?) We lived in it two winters with limited heat from a propane heater we used sparingly. The third winter we hooked up an extension cord and used a small electric heater, mostly to help us get out of bed. That's where I taught myself a little trick. My mummy sleeping bag was nylon so it was very cold to get into in just my underwear. I learned to lie still and use my mind to run a wave of warmth down my body. That kept me warm till my bag warmed up. Now I thought that was clever until I just read about a guy who packed himself in ice for one hour and twelve minutes.

What I do know is that the mind is really powerful and he certainly proved that again to me. If he can do that, then think of all the much easier things we can do if we set our mind to it.

The next five years in Aspen were filled with

many adventures. We had no phone so my buddy would stop in town on his way somewhere. "Want to go to Michigan with 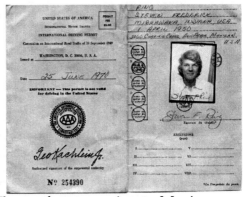 me?" Ah…sure. "Three of us are going to Mexico, can you come?" Ah…sure. I hitchhiked to Arizona and back and forth to Michigan several times, usually with twenty bucks. Only enough for food one-way.

One summer my brother and I left Aspen on

our bicycles with one plan. Stay gone all summer and camp out every night. We rode to Canada but they wouldn't  let these two hippies in because we didn't have one hundred dollars between us. We rode to the ocean, then south to California and visited our other brother there. It was late October before we returned. We came up a little short of making it home to Aspen because it snowed all night. We simply could not ride in a foot

of snow. We hitched a ride. There is no way I would have done all these things if I had listened to the many reasons I shouldn't. I would have missed out on some great memories I treasure.

Stop and think if this is an event (no matter how small) or an adventure worth doing. Take your time, sit down and close your eyes. Then talk yourself into it, rather than out of it.

While we were in Aspen, my brother met someone who was starting a taxicab service. We were immediately drawn to the name, Mellow Yellow Taxi. We would fit right in! We bought an old checker cab from them for $250. Oil change, tune up, clean up and it was okay, except it was black. Of course, it needed to be yellow.

It was spring and still cold, so painting was challenging. We borrowed a one-car garage, put a heater

in it. We painted it outside for a bit, then we'd open the doors real quick and put the car in to dry. We did a section at a time, almost spraying by hand. It took all afternoon to finish. If you didn't look too close, it wasn't too bad. Then we applied the colorful Mellow Yellow door logo, and we were ready for business. Turned out to be an interesting job. When the planes came in we'd charge $1 from the airport to town. We tried to get six in each trip and race back for the next load. That was in the day when Aspen Airways was in business.

I'll never forget the night of a heavy snowstorm. I had a guy who refused to part with one dollar so he walked. It was two miles to town and he was quite a sight trying to carry his skis, boots, poles and suitcase to save that dollar. That's called "carrying it too far" if you know what I mean.

The 70's was the heyday of the ski bum. It was still possible then to work odd jobs or low paying jobs, and still afford to ski. That spawned a whole culture of guys and gals there for the joy of skiing. A ski pass was only $250 for unlimited skiing for the season and you could make six dollars

an hour working. Housing costs were still reasonable (especially for us at zero cost). That allowed us to work in the summer for just enough money

to see us through the ski season. Sometimes I didn't work all of the summer so I had to get a ski pass another way. Why don't I teach skiing? I joined the Aspen ski school orientation and selection process. It was five days of skiing with school reps.

They evaluated your skiing and your personality to see if you were a fit. It was nerve wracking because the style of skiing they taught was totally different than the Michigan style. They taught skis apart, face downhill and no shoulder turn. I honestly did not get it until the last day when we had to ski down a short slope in front of the Ski School Director. I guess I did okay. They asked me to join and I did. Yippee, a free ski pass! But they actually wanted me to teach skiing? I reluctantly did sometimes, especially during the busy times when I had no choice. I liked to teach kids. They learn faster and they're more fun. They called me by my nickname "Ringo". I enjoyed it when I did it. Every day we had to report for work, if there weren't

enough students, I could go off skiing. Everyone lined up in front of the head of our section, the eager to work, right in front of the supervisor. Me in the back, often facing away, making it clear I didn't mind not working. My job was to ski as much as I could. I didn't want her interfering with my job.

When I needed a vacation from my heavy winter work schedule, we would go to Snowbird, Utah for a change of skiing scenery. Times were tough. We were young so we could handle it!

I was lonely. I didn't meet people easily and that means women too. What was I going to do? I didn't like bars so I had to find where the women were. Then it came to me: Woman's softball league. I'll be an umpire! That's how I met my wife. I set out to impress her right away so I took her out to 25¢ beer night. She still liked me! A year and a half

later, she was ready to move closer to family and I was ready for something new. We decided San Diego was close enough to her Los Angeles family. We got married in 1976 and left the next day for San Diego. I'm still married to her. It never would have happened if I hadn't decided to make myself uncomfortable in

the short term (meeting people was hard!), to get what I wanted in the long term.

The best things in life take some effort. We have to be proactive. We have to decide to be happy. Then do what it takes.

Chapter 3 The Path Becomes Clearer

I'd never been to San Diego before, didn't even know anything about it. It was as good a place as any to get a new start. One problem. No jobs. Especially for someone like myself with no skills. Well, not completely. I didn't want to work construction because I didn't want to make a career of it. I didn't see any snow anywhere, so I couldn't teach skiing. In the newspaper, the only section that had a lot of job offerings was sales, especially real estate sales. I guess I'll do that even though it's commission only. I should be okay. I know how to work hard. I'm not so talkative but I'm okay talking to people. Like everyone else, I discovered how really tough the business is. That's why few people became successful at it.

For the first few years I made enough to pay the bills then buy a small condo. A few years later we traded up to a small house when our son was born. I was making just enough. I didn't understand people. I didn't understand the job and my wife was wondering why I worked so much. Does that mean you like working more than you like being with me? Sure, I love working long hours and not making much. I never won those battles, but I wasn't going to lose them either.

Remember, I saw myself as a millionaire (when I was younger) so that vision was stronger than the many obstacles that always appeared in my way. Sometimes I felt like the tortoise, plodding along, always moving, single-mindedly forward. *I was always thinking, what can I do different or better.* You were more likely to catch me with my eyes closed thinking, than you were to catch me watching TV. *I discovered that I had more to gain in the long run, by moving slower and always checking to see if I was headed in the right direction. Time worked to my advantage.*

When my wife and I decided to start a family, she got a lot more interested in sex. Just my luck, she got pregnant right away. This wasn't looking good for me. She got what she wanted. *What's interesting though is how our mind works. When we want an end result, we're willing to do whatever we need to, to get there. Maybe what we have to do is fun, maybe not. Maybe it takes some sacrifice if it isn't fun. Maybe we need to pay more attention, and think more about what is important and we'll be willing to do what's necessary.*

That reminds me of how misguided celebrities can be. They operate without thinking. They feel like the center of the universe. That is until they have a

child, then they suddenly realize they're not. Now they care about their child. ***Why do we have to have a life-changing event to change us and how we think?***

As my son was growing up he played a lot of baseball. I coached his little league team a few times. The boys on the team always had fun. I can't say the same for the parents. They always expected more, demanded more and often refused to keep their emotions in check (or their mouths). Supporting their kids took a back seat to selfishly wanting things their way. The kids easily forgot victories and defeats. (Less by the adults.)

Why are games (we call them that for a reason) so much more important to us as we get *older? They aren't really; we just make them so by how we think about them over and over. We can make anything important if we think about it over and over.*

We had to play one playoff game for the right to represent our suburb in the next round. The team was excited to play our archrivals. The rivals always taunted us and always acted like they were better. They certainly had more talent. We managed to stay even with them the whole game and finally went ahead by one run into the final inning of play. They had runners on every base and were confident they could score and win. After three strikeouts, they lost. I could hardly believe it myself. All my team wanted was to have fun.

All the other team wanted was to win. The other team would have been a better team to go to the playoffs. My kids went and played, but their heart wasn't in it. That was okay, because they had already had their fun. *They were true to what mattered to them. Not what someone else wanted for them. There was no hidden agenda; it was as simple as it should have been. It was all about the fun of doing it. We can learn from kids to enjoy what we're doing. All we need to do is live in the moment.*

I learned a huge lesson in 1984. I wanted to move to a different suburb of San Diego. My wife didn't like to move and only did so if she felt it would greatly improve our lives. I decided the time would come at some point so I set out to prepare. That meant selling a lot more real estate because at 13½% mortgage rates, you needed lots of income to qualify. I saw myself living in this new location so I was willing to do whatever it took. Now remember, I'm still shy and quiet. It was very difficult for me to make myself go out door-to-door and meet strangers. I never liked it. I was never very comfortable. Yet on a regular basis, I went out and worked a territory of about 500 homes. I started having more and more success and I got my income up to a level that was needed to purchase the home I really desired. Then good fortune struck. They closed the

elementary school that was within walking distance of our house. Our son and daughter would have to be driven every day to school. Now my wife was ready and I was ready. We found a house right away and sold our old one. (We are still in that house 25 years later.) We fixed it up and back to work I went.

Within a month I started to notice that I had lost a lot of my motivation to go out and talk to people door to door. I would pull up in the neighborhood and have trouble getting out of the car. Some time elapsed before I realized what happened.

Without dreams and goals there is no motivation that we can sustain. I got my dream and hadn't replaced it with another. I couldn't consciously maintain the motivation.

Life marches on. Now I'm 58 and many things have changed for me over the years. I've worked hard to improve and get better. (So has my wife.) In spite of my shyness, I've learned to be more talkative, speak in front of groups of people and now I really enjoy it. I got an opportunity to manage people and now I've been doing it for 21 years. Twenty of those years, I owned my own real estate offices. It has been rewarding to me and taught me a great deal about people and human nature. ***One thing I've learned is that most people are "too busy" to put much effort into getting better.*** (I hope you're different.)

I've tried to keep my ego under control. I drive a modest car and have stayed in the same home since 1984. That allowed me to pay off the mortgage when I was 50, so we could really relax some. We could have refinanced and spent the money or kept trading up to a bigger house and bigger mortgage, or a more prestigious neighborhood. Instead, I've purchased a number of real estate properties and the tenants are busy paying off the mortgages, and I'm paying lower income taxes too. Every time I have a problem with a property or tenant, I remind myself of those things.

I love being in good physical condition and feeling good. My wife says I still have no rhythm though, even after taking dance lessons. I have to work on that. I feel like I've improved in lots of ways over the years. There are many things I'd still like to do better. (I don't think we should ever stop trying, even if the only thing we're working on is how to improve our ability to talk to people.) That's enough about me.

Now it's your turn!

Chapter 4   Doing the Opposite

*N*ow I'm a thinking, planning-ahead kinda guy. (I learned that sitting on my butt.) I like being prepared, organized. Some things that work when you're young don't work so well anymore. My wife taught me that if you don't plan ahead for a vacation, you don't go. Or if you do go without planning, you get leftovers. (Last room left, last car, worst seat.) When we go to Europe, she starts the planning for the next one while we're there. Our big plan had been to vacation often once both our kids were out and settled. One of our first trips was to France. The media and everyone told us all about the French, how they didn't like Americans and were rude. We decided to see for ourselves and found that not to be true.

We have to form our own opinions based on our own experiences, and when you're nice and friendly, guess what?

I just saw a show about a country in Scandinavia where people are considered to be the happiest of any country. *Apparently, they have reasonable expectations, which most of the time are met and they are therefore happy. Interesting thought. Everyday they think they are content*

and happy and then they are. Good thoughts every day. Interesting!

I'm jealous. I can't seem to get myself to waste money on things that go down in value. (Fancy cars, boats, RV's.) They sure look like fun and they're so easy to get. Why can't I get myself to buy them even when I have the money? Lots of people get stuff and they have no money. What's wrong with this picture? (My rule of thumb is... you can afford the toys when your retirement is fully funded, you have a year of income in the bank and you could pay for them without straining.) Are people having more fun than me? Well, maybe a little. The problem is most people overdo it. (It's expensive to impress yourself and others.) Financially they're okay until something goes wrong and it usually does. If not in the short term, it sure does in the long run. I read about people every day that can barely make it on their social security or retirement income. For many, a little sacrifice in the past might have done wonders for their future. They thought things would turn out just fine without any thought or effort on their part. Wrong! *If you leave your life to chance, then you probably won't end up happy with where you end up.*

Both you and I probably know a bunch of people that are not where they want to be at this point in their lives. They hoped and expected things to be better or

different. The problem was they lived unconsciously. Life has a momentum of its own and it takes over. We put out fires every day. All we're doing is reacting. We do things without really much thought every day. Before we know it, a day, a month, a year has gone by. Our future is unpredictable because it's all left up to chance. We live our life without thinking. When we do get something in our head, it's usually negative. You want to get a divorce or break up? It's easy. (People do it all the time.) Simply tell yourself how unhappy you are, every day. *If you do it well and consistently, you'll be successful in a few months. Don't try to rush it or force it. Patience is a virtue and it will reward you. Good or bad.*

I play a lot of tennis each week. I'm struggling to improve my balance and stability. It struck me that this was the same problem a lot of people have and it leads to inconsistent results. There were times when I've been out of balance and worked too much. I also see a lot of people that don't work much at all. Either way it's not good for you. Or maybe you move fairly often, each time thinking it will make you happier. Maybe it does in the short term. I just read about a guy who inherited some money, bought a BMW then lost his house in foreclosure the same year. The elusive search for happiness and satisfaction.

When our thoughts and mind-set aren't right, no

amount of money or houses or cars or toys will work in the long run. Has anyone tried stability and security first, then toys? How about getting the future covered. Maybe it's not so great to spend everything you make.

Living in the past hurts. All those bad things that happened to us or bad things people did to us. Anytime something reminds us of one of those things, it's hard not to rehash it over and over. I have had a few that worked for me that routinely asked me, "Don't you remember when so and so did that to me?" My answer is usually no. I don't want it taking up space in my head. It's all negative anyway. So far, *I haven't met anyone that can keep negative and positive thoughts at the same time. I'm into positive thoughts–hoping for the best and expecting it. How can something ever come true if in your mind you don't think it can?*

Our mind has a habit of distorting reality or our perception of reality. Our mind wants that perception to conform to our beliefs. Take what we believe to be true or want to be true, then adjust the facts or find only those facts that support our beliefs. Our perception of reality becomes distorted and no one can change our thinking. We become stubborn and uncompromising

in our beliefs, ignoring real facts. For example, it's painful to watch when men or women, about to get married, don't see the problems that all their friends do. Often that potential spouse will not listen or be willing to hear what is so obvious to everyone else. They say that "love is blind" or that people can change.

Well, the truth is, most people don't change because it takes some effort. We just can't be unconscious all the time and hope to do better or get better. There is hope however. This same mind that distorts our perception of reality can be used to change our real reality in a good way.

68   Religion is blind too. Each person establishes their beliefs based on their upbringing or later in life indoctrination. Their perception of reality is then based on their beliefs. No other religion could possibly be correct or have any merit. There is no room for flexibility or other possibilities. Each religious faction would take something like the Bible and look for confirmation of their beliefs. Each one can find what they need to support their beliefs in spite of ample evidence also found that contradicts their beliefs. They just won't recognize or be able to see anything that might disprove what they believe. The lack of flexibility and being able to see the merits in another's position also creates problems in politics. Different belief

systems become polarized, branded and generalized. Compromise is done begrudgingly. *The problem is people lock into their beliefs and whether true or not, their continuous thoughts feed those beliefs (again whether true or not.) Instead of this mind power working unconsciously, we could make a belief of something that we want to be true in the future, then make it come true.* How about doing that instead of fighting with others over religion or politics? Why not make your own dreams come true instead?

Buy Some Real Estate!!

Can I give you some advise? I know what you're thinking, "What the hell do you think you've been doing"? Point taken. Anyway, I'm in the real estate business and I've made my money in real estate. It has also funded college and allowed me to give our kids each a piece of real estate of their own. These things would not have been possible otherwise. Not everyone is comfortable owning real estate other than their own home. Some discomfort can be very rewarding because it makes helping your kids later much easier. You know how hard it is to save money for college. Many parents simply just didn't do it. So now the kids are burdened with student loans for many years. Here's what you

do instead. Buy a duplex, triplex or fourplex to live in first (or a home if you must), then do everything you can to buy one more. Just one condo, house or duplex. The sooner you buy the better because you are on the 15 year plan. Forget about appreciation or depreciation of the value. The only thing you focus on is paying it off in 15 years. When your kids are college age you'll have all you need in equity to fund their schooling. What a nice thing for both of you. What headache would you rather have, no money to help them or some tenant headaches over the years? How about a little sacrifice for the kids? If they don't go to school after all, you have equity to help them buy the real estate they want. I like it because it works!

There are problems everywhere you look. There is so much that can be learned if we pay attention. *Most important, decide to be happy. Don't let how others feel determine how you feel. Don't let their beliefs or what they say alter your course. You need to be on a mission to be happy, to accept what comes your way and make the most of it. Look for what is good in everything and everybody. Be happy for others' success. Enjoy theirs and look for yours at the same time.* If we spent a fraction of the time doing that, (instead of arguing and fighting), we would be amazed at the results. Just think of how much time is spent

each day on negative junk. Now imagine what a few minutes each day focusing on being happy, would do. Bottom line for most people, do the opposite of what they're doing. It would be so much nicer for them and everyone around them.

Chapter 5　Stop and Think

As, a person, if you're not getting a little better every day, you're getting worse. If you're getting worse, how are you going to do better? As we age, our bad habits get worse. We become more and more entrenched in our coping mechanisms and beliefs, more stubborn, less flexible. Is that the way you want to end up? Hopefully not. The solution is to be conscious and work on being better.

Without judgment, begin to ask yourself some questions…

- ❑ I am getting…　better / worse?
- ❑ Am I extra stubborn?
- ❑ Am I depressed?
- ❑ Am I angry?
- ❑ Am I overweight?
- ❑ Am I defensive?
- ❑ Am I prejudiced?
- ❑ Am I an abuser?
- ❑ Is my ego making the decisions?

❑ **Do I jump to conclusions?**

❑ **Am I suspicious of people?**

❑ **Am I a smoker?**

❑ **Am I happy for others?**

❑ **Am I on a mission to be happy?**

❑ **Do I like to fight and argue?**

❑ **Do I love?**

❑ **Am I kind and considerate?**

❑ **Am I expecting the best?**

❑ **Am I paying attention?**

❑ **Am I too busy to get better?**

❑ **Am I full of excuses?**

You can carry this on and on for every positive and negative trait you may have. This process of self-examination can't help but make you better. Could you spare a few minutes a day sitting on your butt and thinking of how to be better? That way you won't unconsciously get a little worse each day. With repetition, our bad habits get worse over time. Think of all those years of practicing the wrong way. It's the unconscious living that gets us in trouble. You must know a bunch of people that are getting worse, not better. Don't be one of them.

It's never too late to be how you want to be. It's never too late to decide to be happy.

Change is difficult. You know that and I know that. It takes lots of effort. I'm going to try to make it easier. I'd like to explain how some things work and I'll also share some tips that have really helped me in my life.

A TIME PLANNER

I was always forgetting things and I see people doing the same every day. Sorry this is so obvious, however most people don't do it: write it down, damn it! Get yourself a planner with a calendar and write things down whenever you think of them. That means keeping it near you. In order to help your conscious mind work better you must free up space. Just like a computer, our brains get bogged down with details and begin to run inefficiently. Think of it as freeing up your mental hard drive. Write down details you think are important: places you need to go, things you need to do, appointments, birthdays and social engagements. Refer to it regularly throughout your day, and use it to plan the next day. Free up your brain. Don't try to remember anything. This will reduce stress and help you to be more efficient. More significantly, it will free up your mind, allowing it to creatively solve problems while you enjoy the moment.

A MEMORY TRICK

Let's improve your memory. Think about how

you remember things. When you remember clearly, it's because you have attached a visual image to what you remember. That's the conscious mind recalling images from your subconscious mind. Without a picture to leave an impression, it stays only in our conscious mind and it's hit or miss to remember. Verbally repeating something to yourself over and over so you will remember it is ineffective. The thought usually gets lost with the thousands of other thoughts floating around in our conscious brain. For the same reason, affirmations repeated over and over are only effective in the short term and to a limited degree. They get lost like everything else. To test out your subconscious memory, picture yourself picking up the laundry two days from now without writing it down. Picture it in your mind, clearly, on that day, driving to the cleaners and picking it up. In two days you'll find yourself doing just that at the time you pictured it. You are predicting your future. Experiment with this concept; try it in other aspects of your life and see how effective it is. Those that have an excellent memory automatically attach pictures without even realizing they're doing it.

BUILT IN ALARM CLOCK

Your subconscious works 24 hours a day, with a built-in internal clock. Before you go to bed, close you eyes and picture yourself waking up, sitting up in

bed, looking at the clock at exactly____a.m. (visualizing a time 15 minutes before you normally wake up) and getting out of bed. Your subconscious should wake you up at the exact time you pictured. In my experience, this will work the first time for about 90% of people. (For the other 10%, the conscious mind gets in the way.) If you are one of those 10%, just keep trying. This is infallible and it will ultimately work for you as well.

Let's start. Write everything down and what you can't write down, use our memory trick. Now I want you to be conscious of some other things that can help. Next time you say, "I don't have the time," remember that means it wasn't as important as everything else you were doing. Stop and think, should it be? Is it important to me? **All I'm asking you to do is stop and think.**

KNOW WHERE YOU'RE HEADED

I had some kidney stones a while back. I guess I wasn't drinking enough water. Sometimes I would unconsciously go my whole work day and not drink. Not good. So, I worked at being more conscious, yet it wasn't enough. Many of you already know how to fix this because the diet programs tell you how. I never drank enough until I took a water bottle and told myself I had to drink it every workday between 10am-2pm. That worked, but then I didn't drink enough on the weekends. There's an important lesson here that

we can apply to our lives with unbelievable results. *By clearly defining (goals) what we want to accomplish and by when, it is much easier to make it happen.*

When I didn't fill my bottle on the weekend it rarely got done. This simple process is so effective that it literally changes people's lives every day.

With the end result in mind, we march towards it every day. We often don't even realize it's happening as the movement can be slow like a tortoise. To have success in any area of your life, you have to know where you want to end up. If you don't care where you end up, then live unconsciously. The thing we know for sure is that you'll end up somewhere.

I want to review the importance of knowing where you're going. Of knowing what you want. The clearer you are, the more likely it will happen. You are definitely not too busy to figure your goals out and write them down. *Your subconscious has no idea where you want to go, and can't help you, if you don't know yourself. It is critical for having the success you want.* You have to give your goals life and energy. You can by thinking about your goals every day. Even for a few minutes. This part is much more important than having a plan of how you will achieve them. That can come gradually over time.

I DON'T HAVE TIME

I don't have time for (or I'm too tired for) sleep, sex, to eat right, to read, to stretch or to exercise. Remember what I said? That's just an excuse. *You're saying other things are more important. Are you really sure? Have you really thought about it or are you unconscious? These things are important for our well-being. What good are you to others if you don't take care of yourself? Once you decide something is important to you, you'll find the time. You can always find the time.* The experts say that 7 – 8 hours of sleep is a healthy amount for the average person. Think of the extra time you might gain right there. You might even give up some sleep for sex. You need that 2 – 3 times a week. (The experts tell me). Remember the doctor sez it also lessens the risk of prostate cancer so you have a duty to help your man.

TEMPTATION

I hate temptation. It means you constantly have to make decisions. It's so much easier if you remove all the temptation you can. It's sure a lot less stressful. For example, I love chocolate. It's the last thing I need laying around. If I need to lose weight, I need to make it easier to eat well rather than to buy something easy. People laugh at me because for years I've taken a bagel and

an apple for lunch. And water. When I don't take it, I get hungry and look for something easy which usually means not too good for me. It takes me 2 minutes to make my lunch or at least 20 minutes to buy something bad for me. I'd rather use the 18 minutes to walk, to think, to play, to enjoy. They say everyone should at least walk if they can't exercise more strenuously. Isn't it funny how we avoid it by habit? We always park as close as we can to where we are going so we don't have to walk. Even going to the gym, everyone parks as close as they can. Go figure.

SAD AND BLUE

What do you do when you're sad, blue, depressed or unhappy? You keep thinking about the things that bother you, or all the bad things happening in your life at the moment. Sometimes it's pretty hard to avoid those feelings, even for the happiest people. We know it's going to happen to us, so let's get ready and practice avoidance. Think and expect good things to happen. That way we can cause those times to be less and less frequent and shorter in duration.

We've got to know what makes us happy, what we are grateful for. If you can't find lots of things, you might be a mess. Use this book, go get some help and start recognizing the many wonderful things in your life. First of all you're alive, right? (If not, why

does your butt hurt so much right now?) How about when you're feeling good, you make a list of every little thing you could possibly be grateful for. Then when you're blue, pull it out, read it over. ***How can you think of the bad things when you're reading and thinking of the good things? There is only so much room in your head. Fill it with the positive.***

Hope you've enjoyed the journey so far. Have you been sitting on your butt reading this the whole time? Is your butt numb? Then stand up, take a break and stretch.

Okay, now it's time to get to work.
It's business time!

Chapter 6 Finish What You Start

*L*et's face it, most people don't have discipline. How did those that have it get it and how do they keep it? Discipline comes from having motivation. What motivates us and how does that work? How can I make that work for me? Can I actually sit on my butt and make that work for me?

The mind is an extremely powerful tool when it has a mission. Remember how you constantly thought about that big promotion or car you wanted until you got it? You can learn to put your thoughts to work like that on a regular basis. Understanding how it works is important. Your mind has two parts, the conscious (able to feel and think, awake, intentional) and the subconscious (occurring with little or no conscious perception). We often say someone is unconscious of what they are doing, they are unaware, not thinking. The subconscious mind has taken over.

THE CONSCIOUS MIND

The conscious thinking part of the mind is really working productively only about 8 hours a day. The other 16 hours are spent sleeping and goofing off. The conscious brain has very little motivation or

will power, except in short bursts. You could say it acts like a teenager, impulsive and impatient, often difficult to manage. *That's why most people don't finish what they start; they can't maintain the motivation it takes by just using conscious willpower.* How many times have you, or someone you know, started a diet and didn't finish? Couldn't maintain the weight after losing some? Started at the gym in January and stopped for the year in February? Old habits die hard they say. We easily fall back to our original patterns. It's frustrating. We mean well. We're really trying hard. It just isn't working. We are trying to consciously force ourselves to do things. Things we want to do and at the same time, don't want to do. Talk about conflict. The *want to's* win in the short term. The *don't want to's* win in the end. We gotta find a way to change that!

THE SUBCONSCIOUS MIND

The other part of our mind, the subconscious, is the opposite of the conscious in many ways. Once something becomes a habit, your subconscious has taken over. Your entire morning routine is probably unconscious. You brush your teeth, get dressed and drive to work without much conscious thought. What's really amazing is that someone can be drunk and still drive. We have short-circuited the conscious mind and

the conscious mind may not remember anything. The subconscious doesn't know it's a bad thing to drive while drunk. In a cruel twist, drunks are usually injured less than their victims in an accident. Their subconscious is relaxed because it doesn't sense fear or danger. The conscious mind of victims does and fights by tensing up. More trusting and childlike, your subconscious accepts whatever it is told without question. This is the part of our mind that advertisers seek to make a connection with. It makes no judgments, doesn't know what is good or bad for you, right or wrong. It is incredibly powerful, the source of intuition, and works 24 hours a day. It can't tell when something is real or make-believe. *Most important of all* *for us to understand, the subconscious is the source of lasting motivation and will power.*

INTUITION

More about the subconscious. The better we understand it, the more we can appreciate its power. *One underrated benefit is intuition. Successful people use it much more than most. It helps to solve problems and come up with solutions.* To use it yourself, gather all the information you can about the situation, then don't try to force a solution. Stop consciously trying. Your subconscious will take over when you are sleeping. It will work in a detached

manner to solve the problem. (It is effective because the conscious mind isn't interfering.) Those solutions will then come to you on the conscious level. You have to pay attention and write them down. Trust this process and you will be rewarded. And here you thought this book was all about sitting on your butt. *Now you know how to change your life while you're sleeping!*

When we don't have time to think, only react, the subconscious kicks in. That's where our habits are stored, as well as our skills. When any advanced level performer has to react there is no time to consciously think of every step. Repetitive practice has locked those steps into their subconscious. It's when we become conscious that things get messed up. The conscious mind can't move fast enough because it analyzes everything. The subconscious is non-judgmental so it can move at lightning speed. The subconscious is our vault. We store everything there. All the good and bad. If we chose to store more negative than positive, then that will determine how we look at life. I have an idea, let's be conscious of what we send for storage. *By systematically planning what goes into our subconscious, we can make meaningful changes in our life.*

OUR MORAL COMPASS
Our subconscious mind can also slow us down.

When we are tempted consciously, it will slow us down if we listen. Like a compass, it points the way. We tend to try to override it, which we can do if it hasn't been set up correctly. *When we have emotionally decided what was important to us, then the subconscious will direct us. If we are unsure or unclear, the subconscious can't help much. Then it's easier to act impulsively and that's usually not good.* What we call our morals are stored in our subconscious, if we are confused about our morals then guess what happens? When children are raised in dysfunctional families, they get confusing signals. Then it's very difficult to have standards of behavior. When there is no remorse, there are no standards. No guidelines exist in their subconscious so everything operates on the conscious, impulsive level. *Our subconscious sits and waits for directions from us. Why not remind it of what's important to us, every day.*

EMOTION
Nothing important was ever accomplished without emotion. Emotion is the fuel that drives the subconscious.

Without the emotion wrapped around the images stored, they are just memories. The motivation and willpower comes from the combination of images

and emotion. The power of that combination cannot be underestimated. If we want changes, we have to take advantage of this power. We already know it doesn't work by using our conscious mind. Why bother. *If we're going to put some effort in to change, let's set ourselves up for success.* Who wants to spend all our time fruitlessly battling with our conscious mind? It is draining and ensures failure. *The subconscious doesn't make you want to do things you don't usually like to do. It just gives you the motivation to do them so you can accomplish the end result you want.*

WHAT HAPPENS IF I'M THINKING GOOD THOUGHTS, BUT BAD THINGS HAPPEN?

You cannot control others or events. You can only control your own reaction to them. You will over time attract people and circumstances that are in tune with your predominate thoughts. How you react while waiting for change to occur will either speed up or slow down change. You must know someone who has a great attitude no matter what happens. That's our goal. Keep expecting good things to happen until they do. This is a process. If it was as simple as wanting good things to happen then it would happen to everyone. You have to believe before it will come true. Your subconscious is there

just for you. It doesn't know what is true or false and it doesn't care. It doesn't care if it's good or bad for you. So your job is to send it continuous messages of happiness and prosperity. It works day and night on your behalf. It will attract positive or negative to you depending on what you tell it over and over. What are you telling yours?

HOW DO I STAY MOTIVATED DURING TRYING CIRCUMSTANCES?

Our subconscious keeps us motivated if we are clear what is important to us. Those things are bigger than one-days, one-months, one-years challenges. Then your subconscious will always be looking past the short-term into the future. It keeps moving toward the future unless you tell it to stop. That would be your conscious mind putting up obstacles. Disbelieving that it could be possible. Focusing on the short-term, the conscious mind will always be in the way of success if you let it. Our lives reflect our predominant thoughts so you can't keep telling yourself things are bad or they won't work. You can make sure things won't turn out well if you keep thinking they won't. You can guarantee your success or failure. Good or bad. I've grown to like the good myself.

WHAT'S WRONG WITH JUST WAITING FOR PEOPLE OR CIRCUMSTANCES TO CHANGE, SO THINGS GET BETTER FOR ME?

Our lives are a reflection of our predominant thoughts. Everything about us now has been determined in the past by those thoughts. Unless we change how we think, nothing around us will change.

What about those people that keep getting divorce after divorce. They are trying to change their circumstances without changing how they think. It doesn't work. You hear of people trying to get a "fresh start" on a new job or a new location. It doesn't work well unless they change how they think. It works sometimes because people are forced to change how they think by the new people around them. When you change your thoughts it changes your attitude. Then your personality starts to change and people around you adapt or leave and you attract new ones. Then gradually everything around you changes.

You are a magnet. Are you putting out negative thoughts and attracting negative thoughts and people? Lots of people are. Don't be one of them. Look for the good, think positively, start attracting the good things you want in your life.

Take charge of your subconscious and you'll be

taking charge of your life. Be conscious of what you are doing and thinking all the time. Don't do this half-assed. Go for it. Believe in yourself. *You are the solution.* If you do nothing, you and only you are the problem. Start now to attract good things into your life by how you think every day.

Before you move onto the next chapter, I have to make sure you appreciate the power of the subconscious mind. If you are unsure if it really works, it would be better for you to go back and read this chapter again. I think it will work better for you if you do. When I show you how to change your life in the next chapter, you'll be more inclined to actually do it, when you believe that it will work for you.

Chapter 7   How to Sit On Your Butt And Direct Your Life

*B*ear with me while we review some important reminders. Remember that *emotion is critical in achieving success.* Over the years, we've all heard of people who had nothing, overcame great odds, and achieved great success. The one thing they all had in common was that they knew, they could see and feel, that they would be successful one day. Their thoughts were energizing, and that energy became powerful enough to create change. We've also heard stories of people who cured themselves of serious medical problems like cancer. They pictured themselves without the tumor and they pictured the emotions they would feel when they heard they were free of cancer. If someone can use the power of their subconscious mind for that, they can use it for all the other things that are important to them.

When positive emotion accompanies each goal or dream, it is absorbed by your subconscious mind. If you look back at your successes, you'll see one common ingredient: positive energy. When you gave up on something, the image of your goal lacked positive emotion. When emotion is added, it acts as rocket fuel. High-powered energy is created and your subconscious

takes off on a mission to accomplish the images it interprets as real. Likewise, past negative emotional experiences exist as pictures in the subconscious and can create more negative experiences. Fortunately, these images are random and unorganized. *We can push them aside by massive daily doses of positive images with emotion.* It is certainly easier than trying to fix issues that control us from our past, which can take many years of dedication to therapy. As we've discussed before, people can't change bad habits like smoking, drinking, or not exercising because they try to solve these problems only on a conscious level. Conscious willpower, however, only motivates them in short bursts. This is why people start and stop bad habits over and over, failing to change time and time again. *Until they add positive emotion to the picture of how they want it to be, they cannot succeed.*

Once you start the process of feeding images with positive emotion, the subconscious will expand into the conscious. All the things you want will pop into your mind frequently. Your motivation skyrockets and you consciously look for more ways to make it work. Gradually, positive images bring your goals closer and closer to you. Some changes happen fast and some will take longer, depending on the strength of the negative images you have stored from your past.

Real change will take 2-3 months or more of concentrated effort. You have to change how you think before any lasting changes will occur in your life. Changing circumstances first rarely works because you have to change how you think for change to last. Waiting for things around you to change before you change how you think doesn't work either. It's only temporary until the next change in circumstances changes how you think again.

The process of changing your life is easier than you think. Could you somehow spare 10 – 20 minutes a day to sit on your butt? The return on your investment is better than you can get anywhere. The only thing that slows down your progress is your judgmental conscious mind. When things aren't going as you had hoped, it will tell you it isn't working. It'll tell you to stop. This will require some persistence in the beginning before the results come. It's important to do this every day. Skipping a day sets you back too much. Hang in there. Don't expect results right away, although small changes will start to occur soon. *Where you are in your life didn't happen overnight so don't expect to change it overnight. Every person is different; your pace of success will be determined by your starting place and how well you do this process. Real change may take 2 – 3 months. Stay with it and you and your subconscious will win.*

Start teaching yourself to focus on the outcome that you want. (By doing this first thing every day you can then focus the rest of the day on living in the moment.) When you believe it will happen, it will change how you think and act. Remember to think big; the only thing holding you back is your doubting conscious mind. It doesn't matter what is in your head now. There are probably lots of negative thoughts already in your vault. They have arrived there over time, without any effort on your part. They tend to be random and disorganized. ***By feeding massive doses of the positive things you want in your life, you'll begin to replace the negative.*** Yes, you need to sit on your butt every day and do this if you want great results. First you have to know what you want.

Current goals are easy. It's much harder to look 10 – 20 years into the future. One of the keys to the process is to know your path. With your future in mind, your subconscious can move towards it. It needs overall direction, the clearer the better. Remember, the subconscious makes no judgments, so tell it where you want to be in your life. I think one of the biggest problems people have is being shortsighted: focusing their whole life on the next few months. This behavior doesn't provide any way to improve and make change possible. Long-term goals are the most important. I

can't emphasize that enough. That's why I want you to figure them out first and work your way back to short term. I like 20 years, however if you're sixty, maybe 10 years seems better to you. I wouldn't do less than 10 years because we need some focus in the distance.

On the next page is a sheet that says, "Things I Am Grateful For." Your first step to having a great life starts here. You need to stop reading and fill that out. You'll feel good when you're done and you'll need it when you start "sitting on your butt." By the way, this list should be long. Don't continue until it is.

THINGS I AM GRATEFUL FOR
(Read this everyday!)

Date: _____

_____

_____

_____

_____

_____

_____

_____

_____

_____

_____

_____

96

_____

_____

_____

_____

_____

_____

_____

_____

_____

_____

_____

_____

THINGS I AM GRATEFUL FOR
(Read this everyday!)

Date:_____

THINGS I AM GRATEFUL FOR
(Read this everyday!)

Date: _____

_____

_____

_____

_____

_____

_____

_____

_____

_____

_____

100 _____

_____

_____

_____

_____

_____

_____

_____

_____

_____

_____

101

On the next page is an example of a 20-year "My Best Life" worksheet. Notice how each sentence is written as a fact. You must follow that method for it to be effective. Your subconscious believes it's true if you tell it it is. So tell it it is!

Notice also the sentences are simple and concise. That will make it easier for you when you use this. There is a blank sheet for you to fill in for yourself on the page after. Then you can move on and do your own sheets for 15, 10, 5, 3, 1 year and shorter, if life is pressing in on you right now.

There is an example for each of those years. Notice how some things change as time goes on. As the years pass, your needs and desires will change so you just change your "My Best Life" worksheets. Take your time to fill these out. It's important and the results will be very rewarding.

MY **BEST** LIFE
BY SITTING ON MY BUTT

Remember: To get what you want and succeed in life, you must be crystal clear. The long-term goals are the most important. Start with them first and work down to the short-term goals. (For example, 20 years down to 3 months) Read a sentence, close your eyes, picture it and *feel it with emotion*.

\# of Years (months) _____ **20** _____ Age: _____

Actual Date_____(maybe your birthday)

Personal
"What is to be"

I am so happy and grateful
I am a patient person.
I am excellent at time management
I am always organized and get important things done right away. I am stress-free and worry free no matter how much I have to do. I am positive and optimistic. I like myself and people like me. I go on vacations whenever I want. I have a long-lasting wonderful and fulfilling relationship with

I always have time for myself and my friends.
I am friendly and I make friends easily.
I always express my feelings clearly and pleasantly.

Financial
"What is to be"   I have more than enough money for everything I want. Money comes easily and frequently.

I have a net worth of $ 10,000,000

I have $ 1,000,000   in the bank

I have $ 30,000   of income coming to me every month.

I live in my own beautiful home with no mortgage.

Physical
"What is to be"   I weigh 130 lbs, I'm perfectly healthy, and physically fit, always energetic.

Spiritual
"What is to be"   I am always at peace.

I donate $

to charity every month.

I regularly volunteer some of my time to those in need.

MY BEST LIFE
BY SITTING ON MY BUTT

Remember: To get what you want and succeed in life, you must be crystal clear. The long-term goals are the most important. Start with them first and work down to the short-term goals. (For example, 20 years down to 3 months) Read a sentence, close your eyes, picture it and _**feel it with emotion.**_

# of Years (months) _____ Age: _____
Actual Date_____(maybe your birthday)

Personal
"What is to be"

Financial
"What is to be"

_____

_____

_____

_____

_____

_____

_____

_____

Physical
"What is to be"

_____

_____

_____

_____

Spiritual
"What is to be"

_____

_____

_____

_____

_____

_____

_____

MY **BEST** LIFE
BY SITTING ON MY BUTT

Remember: To get what you want and end up where you want to end up, you must be crystal clear. The long-term goals being the most important. Start with long-term goals first and work down to the short-term goals. (For example, 20 years down to 3 months) Read a sentence, close your eyes, picture it and <u>feel it with emotion.</u>

# of Years (months) _____**10**___ Age: _____
Actual Date_____(maybe your birthday)

Personal I am so happy and grateful.
"What is to be" I am a patient person.

I am excellent at time management
I am always organized and get important things done right away. I am stress-free and worry-free no matter how much I have to do. I am positive and optimistic. I like myself and people like me. I go on vacations whenever I want I have a long-lasting wonderful and fulfilling relationship with

I always have time for myself and my friends.
I am friendly and I make friends easily.
I always express my feelings clearly and pleasantly.

Financial
"What is to be" I have more than enough money for everything I want. Money comes easily and frequently. I have a net worth of $ 5,000,000

I have $ 500,000 in the bank.

I have $ 25,000 of income coming to me every month. I live in my own beautiful home with no mortgage.

Physical
"What is to be" I weigh 130 lbs., I'm perfectly healthy and physically fit, always energetic.

Spiritual
"What is to be" I am always at peace. I donate $_____ to charity every month.

I regularly volunteer some of my time to those in need.

MY **BEST** LIFE
BY SITTING ON MY BUTT

Remember: To get what you want and end up where you want to end up, you must be crystal clear. The long-term goals being the most important. Start with long-term goals first and work down to the short-term goals. (For example, 20 years down to 3 months) Read a sentence, close your eyes, picture it and <u>feel it with emotion.</u>

# of Years (months) **5** Age: _____
Actual Date_____(maybe your birthday)

Personal
"What is to be"

I am so happy and grateful. I am a patient person.   I am excellent at time management. I am always organized and get important things done right away. I am stress-free and worry-free no matter how much I have to do. I am positive and optimistic. I like myself and people like me.
I go on vacations whenever I want.
I have a long-lasting wonderful and fulfilling relationship with

I always have time for myself and my friends.
I am friendly and I make friends easily.
I always express my feelings clearly and pleasantly.

Financial
"What is to be" I have more than enough money for everything I want. Money comes easily and frequently.

I have a net worth of $ 2,500,000.

I have $ 250,000 in the bank.

I have $ 25,000 of income coming to me every month.

I live in my own beautiful home with no mortgage.

Physical
"What is to be" I weigh 130 lbs. I'm perfectly healthy and physically fit, always energetic.

Spiritual
"What is to be" I am always at peace. I donate $ _____ to charity every month.

I regularly volunteer some of my time to those in need.

MY **BEST** LIFE
BY SITTING ON MY BUTT

Remember: To get what you want and succeed in life, you must be crystal clear. The long-term goals are the most important. Start with them first and work down to the short-term goals. (For example, 20 years down to 3 months) Read a sentence, close your eyes, picture it and <u>feel it with emotion.</u>

# of Years (months) _____3_____ Age: _____
Actual Date_____
(maybe your birthday)

Personal
"What is to be"

I am so happy and grateful. I am a patient person. I am excellent at time management

I am always organized and get important things done right away.
I am stress-free and worry-free no matter how much I have to do. I am positive and optimistic.
I like myself and people like me. I go on vacations whenever I want. I have a long-lasting wonderful and fulfilling relationship with

I always have time for myself and my friends. I am friendly and I make friends easily. I always express my feelings clearly and pleasantly.

Financial
"What is to be"

I have more than enough money for everything I want. Money comes easily and frequently.

I have a net worth of $

I have $ in the bank.

I have $ of income coming to me every month.

I live in my own beautiful home with no mortgage.

Physical
"What is to be"

I weigh 130 lbs, I'm perfectly healthy and physically fit, always energetic.

Spiritual
"What is to be"

I am always at peace.

I donate $ to charity every month

I regularly volunteer some of my time to those in need.

MY BEST LIFE
BY SITTING ON MY BUTT

Remember: To get what you want and succeed in life, you must be crystal clear. The long-term goals are the most important. Start with them first and work down to the short-term goals. (For example, 20 years down to 3 months) Read a sentence, close your eyes, picture it and <u>feel it with emotion.</u>

# of Years (months) _____/_____ Age: _____
Actual Date_____ (maybe your birthday)

Personal
"What is to be"

I am so happy and grateful.
I am a patient person. I am
excellent at time management

113

I am always organized and get important things done right away. I am stress-free and worry-free no matter how much I have to do. I am positive and optimistic. I like myself and people like me. I go on vacations whenever I want. I have a long-lasting wonderful and fulfilling relationship with

I always have time for myself and my friends. I am friendly and I make friendseasily. I always express my feelings clearly and pleasantly.

Financial
"What is to be" I have more than enough money for everything I want. Money comes easily and frequently.

I have a net worth of $

I have $ _____ in the bank.

I have $ _____ of income coming to me every month.

I live in my own beautiful home with no mortgage.

Physical
"What is to be" I weigh 130 lbs, I'm perfectly healthy and physically fit, always energetic.

Spiritual
"What is to be" I am always at peace.

I donate $ _____ to charity every month.

I regularly volunteer some of my time to those in need.

Remember: To get what you want and succeed in life, you must be crystal clear. The long-term goals are the most important. Start with them first and work down to the short-term goals. (For example, 20 years down to 3 months) Read a sentence, close your eyes, picture it and <u>feel it with emotion.</u>

\# of Years (months) _____ Age: _____

Actual Date _____(maybe your birthday)

Personal
"What is to be"

Financial
"What is to be"

_____

_____

_____

_____

_____

_____

_____

_____

Physical
"What is to be"

_____

_____

_____

_____

_____

Spiritual
"What is to be"

_____

_____

_____

_____

_____

_____

_____

MY BEST LIFE
BY SITTING ON MY BUTT

Remember: To get what you want and succeed in life, you must be crystal clear. The long-term goals are the most important. Start with them first and work down to the short-term goals. (For example, 20 years down to 3 months) Read a sentence, close your eyes, picture it and <u>feel it with emotion.</u>

# of Years (months) _____ Age: _____

Actual Date_____(maybe your birthday)

Personal
"What is to be"

Financial
"What is to be"

_____
_____
_____
_____
_____
_____
_____
_____

Physical
"What is to be"

_____
_____
_____
_____
_____

Spiritual
"What is to be"

_____
_____
_____
_____
_____
_____
_____
_____

MY BEST LIFE
BY SITTING ON MY BUTT

Remember: To get what you want and succeed in life, you must be crystal clear. The long-term goals are the most important. Start with them first and work down to the short-term goals. (For example, 20 years down to 3 months) Read a sentence, close your eyes, picture it and <u>feel it with emotion.</u>

# of Years (months) _____ Age: _____

Actual Date_____(maybe your birthday)

Personal
"What is to be"

Financial
"What is to be"

_____
_____
_____
_____
_____
_____
_____
_____
_____

Physical
"What is to be"

_____
_____
_____
_____

Spiritual
"What is to be"

_____
_____
_____
_____
_____
_____
_____

Okay numb butt, this is the simple part. You've worked hard to decide how you want your life to be from here on. Now you take those sheets you filled out and retire to a quiet place where you won't be disturbed for 10 – 20 minutes. (I do it first thing in the morning when I get up.) This is the real beneficial "sitting on your butt." Go ahead, sit on it and relax. Read your "I Am Grateful For" list. Savor it for a couple of minutes. Now move on to your longest-away goal (10 – 20 years) and work your way back to the present. Read the first sentence, close your eyes, picture it and *feel the emotion* as if it's true. (That's what makes it real to the subconscious.) Repeat the process with each sentence on its own. Then go on to the next (15 – 5 etc.) sheet down to the present.

Do this every day. That's all there is to it. You are now feeding massive doses of positive things you want to happen to your subconscious. Before long, you will push aside the negative images and thoughts that reside there.

You can fix anything, change anything this way, but you must do it consistently to get the best results. If you find yourself trying to take on too much, you may stop doing it regularly. Better to cut back on the number of items on your list to change, then to cut back doing this every day. Do something every day, even if it's just working on one thing. You can use this

technique for small changes in your life as well. For example, you could make yourself comfortable asking someone for a date and see yourself feeling good no matter what the response. You could see yourself giving a speech, enjoying it and having the audience respond favorably. You can use this for any number of short-term challenges. *Just decide what you want, picture doing it, add the emotion and it will happen.*

Some people have trouble visualizing an image. It may help to cut out pictures of how you'd like to look, a car you want, a house, or a vacation. Some call it a vision board. You can look at it, close your eyes and imagine the emotions you'll feel when the goal is attained. *It can be very helpful to picture yourself talking to others.* For example, picture the doctor telling you that you are in perfect health, a friend commenting on how great you look, how patient you have become, or how great you are at time-management. Have those complimentary conversations and experience the positive feelings.

It may not work for you right away, just keep practicing. To get meaningful results, you must do this daily for 2-3 months or more. Any less will risk falling back to old thinking patterns; (that's why you can't ever stop your new thinking). Envision a clear image and experience the positive feelings. It will work, don't

give up. This process will address many problems you may have, such as smoking, drinking, drugs, poor finances, gambling, anger, jealousy, envy, weight, procrastination, stress and worry. Don't let these things control your life. Don't accept that you can't change them. Just telling yourself over and over that "you can't" is damaging. Change the thought patterns with this process. Change your life. (If you are using this process to lose weight, don't get on a scale until you feel you are the weight you pictured.) For a little more help in how to picture your desires, see "The Process."

THE PROCESS

Read **"What is to be"** then close your eyes and imagine **"the picture I see."**
(**Remember:** the most important part is experiencing the feeling when you picture it.)
Me in 20 years on my birthday...

A) Personal:

1. **What is to be:** *I am grateful and happy.*
   The picture I see: *I feel happy all the time and remember the moments that cause those feelings of happiness.*

2. **What is to be:** *I am enthusiastic.*

   The picture I see: *Whenever I am around people I see myself upbeat and excited. People love being around me.*

3. **What is to be:** *I have a long-term mutually satisfying relationship with my partner and they have the 5 qualities that I find most important... (list them here).*

   The picture I see: *The person having these 5 qualities; we are happy and in love and how that makes both of us feel.*

B) Financial:

1. **What is to be:** *I own my own home with no mortgage.*

   The picture I see: *Sitting in my dream house, looking around and feeling pride, security, peace. I pick up a piece of paper on the table that says "mortgage" across the top of it and read the big bold red letters diagonally across the page that says "PAID IN FULL."*
   I experience the satisfaction and comfort that would accompany this achievement.

2. **What is to be:** *I get a check in the mail each month for $10,000.*

   The picture I see: *I walk to the mailbox on the 1st of each month, look through the mail until I find the letter I want. I open it and inside is a check made out to me for*

*$10,000. In the memo box it says "January Payment,"
then February Payment" etc. every month of the year.
Experience the way this would feel.*

3. **What is to be:** *I have $1,000,000 in the bank.*
   The picture I see: *I open the mail once a month and
   find my bank statement showing $1,000,000.
   Experience the feelings you will have.*

4. **What is to be:** *I go on vacations whenever I want.*
   The picture I see: *I write out a check for whatever
   airline tickets cost, without a second thought or
   hesitation. I write a check for a hotel for whatever the
   cost without a hesitation. Experience feeling no concern
   at all over the cost, just the enjoyment of it.*

C) Physical

1. **What is to be:** *I weigh ____ lbs. I'm perfectly healthy
   and physically fit. I'm energetic.*
   The picture I see: *I see myself getting on the scale and
   weighing ____ lbs., and feeling great! I eat healthy food
   in moderation. Others tell me how great I look and I do
   look great!*

2. **What is to be:** *I have no pain and I am perfectly healthy.*
   The picture I see: *I move around effortlessly and am*

*pain-free. My doctor tells me I am completely healthy.
I experience the confidence and gratitude for my health.
I see myself doing the physical activities I've always
wanted to do or that I previously haven't been able to do.
I see myself playing tennis, hiking, or biking and feeling
great.*

D) Spiritual

1. **What is to be:** *I volunteer 2 hours every day to help the
   needy.*
   The picture I see: *I help others and it makes me feel
   really good.*

2. **What is to be:** *I donate money every month to a number
   of charities.*
   The picture I see: *I give money to my favorite charities
   every month and experience appreciation and satisfaction.*

E) More Ideas

1. **What is to be:** *I am a non-smoker.*
   The picture I see: *Whenever and wherever I used to
   smoke cigarettes, I see myself enjoying those activities
   even more now without smoking. Others keep telling me
   how great it is that I've quit.*

2. **What is to be:** *I enjoy making sales calls.*
   The picture I see: *I always feel good when making those calls and customers always respond well to what I say.*

3. **What is to be:** *I like my job and the people I work with.*
   The picture I see: *I enjoy everyone I work with including my supervisors. Our communication is always upfront and honest.*

4. **What is to be:** *I have a pleasant, fulfilling relationship with* _____
   The picture I see: *I always enjoy* _____
   *company and it is very satisfying to both of us. These are the things I love and appreciate about him/her*_____

   _____

5. **What is to be:** *I always find time for myself and my family.*
   The picture I see: *I do the things I love to do on a regular basis. I feel re-energized and renewed.*

6. **What is to be:** *I always get a restful night's sleep.*
   The picture I see: *I wake up each morning feeling rested and refreshed, eager to tackle the day.*

7. **What is to be:** *I am a non-drinker.*

The picture I see: *Whenever and wherever I used to drink alcohol, I now see myself enjoying those activities even more without drinking. I see myself repeatedly saying, "No, thank you, I'm happy." I avoid heavy drinkers. Others tell me how much more they enjoy my company when I don't drink.*

8. **What is to be:** *I drink alcohol in moderation.*
   The picture I see: *I drink infrequently and very little when I do and I am satisfied. I only enjoy the company of those who drink in moderation.*

9. **What is to be:** *My garage (or workplace etc.) is neat and orderly.*
   The picture I see: *I see my garage as neat and orderly and I feel I am in control of my life and I like it.*

10. **What is to be:** *I love my job.*
    The picture I see: *I see myself in my ideal job, enjoying it every day.*

11. **What is to be:** *I always keep my anger under control.*
    The picture I see: *I see myself getting angry, controlling it in a normal manner and handling myself and others with respect. I communicate my feelings in a healthy way.*

12. **What is to be:** *I am a non-gambler.*

The picture I see: *I see myself enjoying non-gambling activities and using my money constructively. I avoid gamblers and places where there is temptation.*

Finding Someone

How do we use this technique to find someone to share your life with? First you have to figure out what is important to you. This is taking it beyond wishful thinking and hoping. You need to write it down. Combine thinking big with being realistic. The list has to be believable enough to you, so your doubtful conscious mind doesn't keep interfering and making it more difficult. Caveat: It will do that anyway. Now your subconscious will know what to look for and it will do that 24 hours a day. Isn't that easier than consciously hoping for someone once in a while? Consciously review your list regularly. Think about it, picture that person appearing and you having a mutually rewarding and fulfilling relationship. Use the positive emotion of that experience, rather than a negative emotion focusing on the fact you don't have the person in your life now. *Sometimes to find better, you have to get better. When you get better, better will appear.*

Losing Weight

You've been trying to lose weight, nothing is

working. It doesn't make sense to keep signing up for diet programs. Don't waste your money. When your thinking is right, then having a diet plan will work. The first step is to get a clear idea of what your ideal weight would be. It needs to be realistic. A weight that you believe others would consider a normal weight for your age and size. Think about the anorexic. They use their mind to focus on an (unhealthy) weight, always picturing that they are too heavy. They are using their subconscious in an unhealthy manner. You can use yours to get healthy results. You see yourself being the weight you want, picturing how happy you are and see yourself being complimented by others. Again, the emotion you attach to the weight is the key. You don't need to weigh yourself nor do you want to. You don't want your conscious mind looking at the scale and saying it isn't working. Your conscious mind will be the biggest problem. Stay away from the scale. Give your subconscious the best chance of success.

Get the house you want. Get the job you want. Can you picture them? You have to help your subconscious out. It needs direction. Write it down and be specific. The better you can "see it" the better the results. How would you feel when those things were true in your life? That's the feeling you want to create every day, and feel it when you're visualizing the picture of it. Adding the emotion to the picture gives it the power to make

it happen. Remember that nothing happens overnight. Good things require effort and perseverance. The results you want aren't free, so give this process the effort it deserves. When your subconscious knows where you want to go, it will take you there. Give it a chance to perform.

How's the experience going? Trouble getting yourself to do it? Trouble maintaining the motivation? Then you're fighting this thing on the conscious level every day. It's a tough battle that way. It takes tremendous will power and energy to get yourself to do it each time. And you'll lose as much as you'll win. Over time it will get harder and harder to get yourself to do it until you just stop. That is until the next year's resolution, or some doctor says your life depends on it. The key is to use the power of your subconscious to do the work. Once set up and maintained, it works hard for you. And you'll find you don't have to fight the daily battle. This process may not make you enjoy exercising any more; it gives you the motivation to get it done. What is the big thing, the big goal you want to accomplish by exercising? Just to be in better shape? Feel better? Then what exactly does that look like or feel like. That's what your subconscious needs. How do you think a body builder does it? They are locked in emotionally to a picture of what they want to look like. Do the same.

Sex

I'm a fan of sex, so it's hard to understand why someone isn't. I guess there can be lots of reasons. If you'd like to be more interested in sex then you are, read on. If not that's okay unless you have a partner that is interested in sex. Neglecting their interest could be a problem in the long run. Men and women who are unfulfilled, seek outlets elsewhere. Although you may have no interest in sex, having a mutually satisfying relationship may require effort beyond your current comfort zone. Right now, you probably tell yourself over and over that you don't like sex, it's no fun, it's uncomfortable, it's a chore, I don't have time, I'm too tired, I'm too cranky. For starters, you have to picture that sex is important for a healthy relationship. You look forward to sex and you always enjoy it. You have to attach positive emotion to those pictures. With repetition, they will replace the negative one you repeat to yourself now. So lay down and have some fun and have a satisfying relationship with your partner.

Coffee

It doesn't seem like many people want to give up coffee drinking. If you do, then you have to start telling yourself you don't like it. Get that mental picture going of you not liking the taste or smell. Have a negative

reaction to it. See yourself getting something else to drink when you normally would have coffee. Imagine others saying, "You're the smart one," "I'm proud of you," or "I wish I could quit" and how good that makes you feel. It won't be long and you'll be done with coffee.

Smoking or Drugs

You can use the same method with smoking. Every day you tell yourself you don't like it. Don't like the taste or smell. See yourself avoiding the smoking spots where you usually go to puff. Break the bond between smoking, drinking and the social aspect of it. Picture yourself being sickened by smoking and not feeling very well every time you touch a cigarette. See yourself getting compliments and how that makes you feel so good. Others are proud of you. Soak it in. See yourself saying, "No thanks," whenever offered a cigarette. (Substitute the word drugs for smoking.) Create new habits by telling your subconscious what you want.

You'll have all you want in life if you take 10 – 20 minutes a day to do these exercises. It's not difficult. Your life can begin to change just by having written down your long-term goals and thinking about them all the time. If your life is stagnant, then imagine what you want while focusing on the positive emotion. It

is an irresistible combination and you'll find that the things you seek are seeking you. You can begin to control your life. It can be an amazing life. In this process, you can foresee your future – *what is to be* for you. You create a future that will fulfill you. Others may say how "lucky" you are and that things just seem to come your way. You can be stress-free, worry-free, and at peace. You can have wonderful, fulfilling relationships. You can be financially secure. It's time for you to get your fair share of happiness and prosperity, and share them with others in turn.

May you have love, health and wealth. May you be conscious of the trail you are on and where it is taking you. May you enjoy the journey and the adventures along the way. Happy trails to you.

Right now is an important moment.

Notes

Personal
"What is to be"

Financial
"What is to be"

Physical
"What is to be"

Spiritual
"What is to be"

Personal

"What is to be"

138

Financial
"What is to be"

_____

Physical
"What is to be"

Spiritual
"What is to be"

Personal
"What is to be"

140

Financial
"What is to be"

_____
_____
_____
_____
_____
_____
_____
_____

Physical
"What is to be"

_____
_____

141

_____
_____
_____

Spiritual
"What is to be"

_____
_____
_____
_____
_____
_____
_____

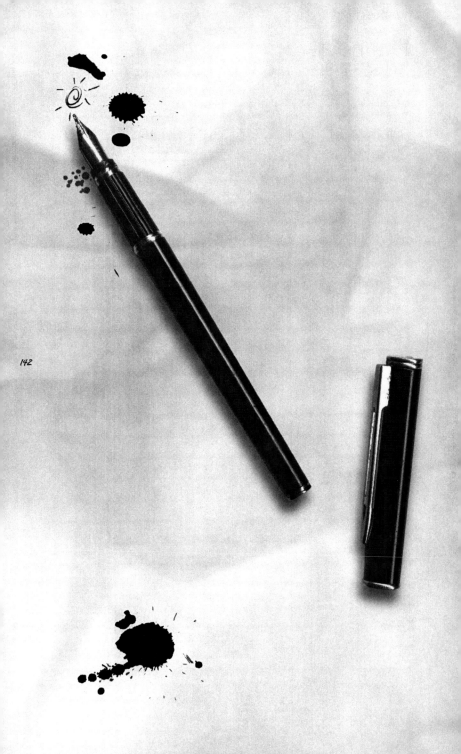

A Quick Summary of Tips

1

Be happy and enjoy yourself no matter what you are doing.
You decide what happiness is for you, not someone else.

2

Don't be too busy to enjoy the good moments along the way.

3.

Pay attention to what you are doing. You'll get better results.
It's easier to get better and improve.

4.

Holding thoughts in your head over time makes them come true.
Some regular quiet time alone is a good thing.
You end up getting what you want.

5.

Sitting on your butt works better than exercising, because it's all
about what's in your head.
Everything you accomplish always starts there.

6.

Life is not always fair and the only thing you can control is your
reaction to what happens.

7.

By sitting on your butt quietly and relaxing, you can come up
with ideas and think creatively. Your mind works better.

8.

How you think about things, what you believe you can do,
has a huge effect on what ends up happening.

9.

Be honest and be fair.

10.

Don't let your ego decide what's important. It will cost you money and it will slow down your personal development. The things you do for your ego only make you feel good temporarily.

11.

Don't try to control everything. There are usually a number of good ways to do things. Remain flexible, you'll live longer.

12.

When you can picture being or having something before it becomes a reality, you're well on your way to making it come true.

ing
13.

Some of your best times are when you are not in a hurry.

14.

You can put up with pain and discomfort if there is something more important to you. When you want something badly enough, you will do whatever it takes. Control this energy to make your dreams come true.

15.

Your emotions create motivation that far surpasses what you can generate by consciously trying.

16.

Ask yourself if you will ever have a chance for an adventure like this again. Little one or big one.
These are the times you will remember.

17.

The mind is really powerful. What people have been able to do is incredible. You can achieve greatness with small things too if you set your mind to it.

18.

The best things in life take some effort. You have to be proactive. You have to decide to be happy. Then do what it takes.

19.

Keep checking on yourself. Can you do better or do it differently? Are you headed in the right direction? Time will work to your advantage if you are focused on what is important to you.

20.

You need to pay attention and think about what is important. When it's important, you'll do what it takes to make it happen. Even sacrifice. Even doing things that aren't that much fun in the meantime.

21.

Don't wait for a life-changing event to force yourself to change. Decide to live now.

22.

You can make anything important if you think about it over and over. You can make things come true.

23.

Live in the moment whenever you can. Enjoy what you're doing or accept what you're doing.

24.

Without dreams and goals, you will not be able to maintain your motivation. Your conscious mind will only sustain you in short bursts before you lose the motivation you need.

25.

Think good thoughts every day. Think you're happy every day, and you will be. Always be conscious of what you are thinking.

26.

If you leave your life to chance, you probably won't end up happy with where you end up.

27.

Patience is a virtue when you are trying to change.

28.

When your thoughts and mind set aren't right, no amount of money or houses or cars or toys will work in the long run. Have you tried stability and security first, then toys? How about getting the future covered. It's not so great to spend everything you make.

29.

Hope for the best and expect it. There is only room for positive or negative thoughts. Chose wisely.

30.

It's worth repeating... Don't leave your life to chance. You probably won't end up happy with where you end up.

31.

You need to be conscious most of the time, that way you can do better and get better.

32.

Decide to be happy. Don't let how others feel determine how you feel. Don't let their beliefs or what they say alter your course. You need to be on a mission to be happy, to accept what comes your way and make the most of it. Look for what is good in everything and everybody. Be happy for others' success. Enjoy theirs and look for yours at the same time.

33.

It's never too late to be how you want to be and it's never too late to decide to be happy.

34.

When you say "I don't have the time,"
it means it's not important as everything else you are doing.
Stop and think… should it be?
Have you really given it the thought it deserves or are you being unconscious?

35.

When you clearly define your goals, what you want to accomplish
and by when, it is much easier to make it happen.
With the end results in mind, you'll march slowly towards it every day.
You live consciously and the success you want becomes yours.

36.

Know what you're grateful for, otherwise the things you're not happy about
occupy your thoughts. Fill your head with the positive.

37.

Nothing important was ever accomplished without emotion.
It is the fuel that drives the subconscious.
Remind your subconscious every day what is important to you.

38.

The subconscious doesn't make you want to do things you don't usually want to do.
It just gives you the motivation to do them so you can accomplish the end
result you want.

39.

You cannot control others or events.
You can only control your own reaction to them.
Set out to improve the situation by your own reaction, not make it worse.

40.

Take charge of your subconscious and you'll be taking charge of your life.
Change how you think, and things will change around you.
You are the solution.

GUIDE TO A BETTER LIFE

Do these every day!

☐   1. Sleep 7 – 8 hours, try going to bed and get up at the same time.

☐   2. Eat a hardy breakfast.

☐   3. Floss and save your teeth.

☐   4. Spend at least 10–20 minutes sitting on your butt as described in this book and dream big (including reviewing what you are thankful for).

☐   5. Stretch.

☐   6. Exercise or walk some.

☐   7. Write everything down.

☐   8. Plan the next day the evening before.

☐   9. Eat healthy, pack your lunch and try not to eat after 7 PM.

☐   10. Have sex regularly.

GUIDE TO A BETTER LIFE

Do these every day!

☐ 11. Enjoy the little things.

☐ 12. Read what you enjoy.

☐ 13. Remain conscious; try to get a little better at something.

☐ 14. Ask for what you want in a nice way.

☐ 15. Remove or distance temptation.

☐ 16. Listen to soothing music.

☐ 17. Have a little fun, laugh a lot.

☐ 18. Be kind and generous and look for the best in everybody.

☐ 19. Expect Health, Wealth and Love.

☐ 20. Remember, until you decide this list is important, you won't find the time.

Live a conscious life.

Notes

Live a conscious life.